YALTA

YALTA

YESTERDAY, TODAY, TOMORROW

Jean Laloy

Translated by

William R. Tyler

A Cornelia & Michael Bessie Book

HARPER & ROW, PUBLISHERS, New York
Grand Rapids, Philadelphia, St. Louis, San Francisco
London, Sydney, Singapore, Tokyo, Toronto

FIRST EDITION

Designed by Karen Savary

Library of Congress Cataloging-in-Publication Data
Laloy, Jean.
  [Yalta. English]
  Yalta: yesterday, today, tomorrow/Jean Laloy; translated by
William R. Tyler.—1st ed.
    p. cm.
  "A Cornelia & Michael Bessie book."
  Bibliography: p.
  Includes index.
  ISBN 0-06-039105-7
  1. Yalta Conference (1945) I. Title.
D734.C7 1990zr
940.53' 141—dc20   89-11145

---

90 91 92 93 94 CC/RRD 10 9 8 7 6 5 4 3 2 1

Contents

Introduction

WHY SHOULD WE concern ourselves with a conference which took place more than forty years ago and lasted only eight days?

Because, after so many months and years our continent does not know real peace. The present status of Europe is a status of fact: to the east, parties that are not only unique but also vassals of the Communist party of the USSR; to the west, liberal regimes with their weak points, but also their treasure—basic freedoms, freedom of the press, free elections, and representative governments.

However, within the Soviet Union as within its European allies, something is beginning to stir. We don't yet know what will come of this. But evolution (not crisis free) does not seem to be out of the question. If this is so, it may be useful to think over the causes of the 1945 partition of Europe. We have attempted to identify these causes by studying the Yalta Conference and its consequences, i.e., the crisis which broke out between the USSR and its allies as early as February 1945 and perpetuated itself through various stages long after victory in the spring. We have tried to find out what it was difficult to avoid, what might

1

have been avoided, and what was desirable. We have formed certain ideas on what was possible and might—why not?—become so again.

But, people will say, Yalta was the division of Europe between the Anglo-Americans and the Soviets. How can we emerge from that dead end? The answer is that there are at least three versions of Yalta: that of the *carving up* of Europe between the superpowers, a version widely accepted in France; that of a liberated Europe longing for *revolution,* a revolution which, thanks to the presence of the Soviet forces, took shape east of the Elbe, whereas to the west it was stifled by the United States, a version current in the USSR; and finally, the opinion held by certain American historians for whom the Crimea Conference (as it is officially called in the USSR) is the model of a good settlement in which claims and concessions cancel each other out according to the rules of *classic diplomacy.*

If we examine these three theses from a critical standpoint, we see that each is based on an assumption which distorts reality: in the first case, that of *carving up,* because no carving up occurred; in the second, the *revolutionary movement* thesis, because this movement, except for Yugoslavia, was manufactured by the Soviet Communist party; finally, in the third, that of *traditional diplomacy,* because what was at stake is not a matter of rivers, forts, or mountain ranges, but the convictions and the fate of millions of human beings. In all three cases, these modes of explanation do not fully take reality into account.

What, in fact, is this reality? In order to ensure peace in the future, Roosevelt wanted to preserve the understanding with Stalin which led to victory. Churchill, concerned by the Soviet advance toward the west, did not always succeed in convincing his powerful American ally. As for Stalin, he acted as though the whole of Europe was to fall under his control: not that Europe should become communist at once! More simply, once the Americans had returned home, the USSR would exert a dominant influence over the entire continent: total influence in the east and growing influence in the west.

Yalta, therefore, was Roosevelt's ultimate effort to preserve the understanding with the USSR. No one today doubts that he was mistaken. He questioned himself on this point a few days before his death, on April 12, 1945. But later, when events belied Roosevelt's hopes, his vain efforts to mollify Stalin facilitated, to a certain extent, the task left to his successors, who were anxious to open a new phase, which started in June 1947 with General Marshall's speech at Harvard University. "The patient," he said, "is sinking while the doctors are arguing." The patient is Europe; the doctors are the four powers administering what remains of Germany.

The patient is not completely cured. But he is improving. He would improve still more were he to make the effort to grasp what occurred at the end of the war. May this little book prove helpful in this task!

Paris, May 1988

1

No Rule in Common

In 1941, THE WAR launched by Hitler changed in character. England, the sole barrier since June 1940, found herself, at the end of the year, flanked by the two greatest powers in the world. This reversal, which rewarded Churchill's tenacity, was above all due to the enemy. After the Japanese attack on Pearl Harbor, Hitler, who had hurled himself at the USSR in June, decided in his turn to declare war on the United States. In the belief that he was preparing for the final showdown with Roosevelt, he himself fashioned the "Grand Alliance," which was to lead Germany to disaster and himself to suicide.

This alliance was based neither on common objectives nor on common convictions. It was due to circumstances. England and France entered the war of their own will, the United States was dragged into the conflict by its growing resistance to Japanese and German expansion. The Soviet Union found itself thrown into it against its will.

Fragile because of its origins, the alliance was even more so because of its composition. It was in fact made up of two alliances. One, between Great Britain and the United States, matured slowly but surely following the

French disaster of June 1940. The other, between these two countries and the Soviet Union, followed suddenly on two years of distrust, not to say pure and simple hostility. The first was based not only on common language, customs, and culture, but notwithstanding often-divergent interests, on a few great ultimate common factors. The second was undermined: to the east by inveterate mistrust and suspicion and to the west by mixed stupefaction and hope—stupefaction because of the strange ally and hope that everything would eventually work out all right.

During the war (we held together because there was no alternative) and peace (each man for himself), the meeting at Yalta (one short week) was a threshold, a typical moment. That which at first had been hailed as the dawn of a new era, in fact revealed itself, after everyone had gone home, as the source of a series of crises, occurring at intervals from February until May 1945; crises followed by lulls, then by renewed tensions, and so on: "an armed truce," as Litvinov[1] said at the time, and not peace.

If we can arrive at an exact understanding of the tendencies and the objectives of each party, then of the nature of negotiations, and finally of their immediate results, we shall perhaps better understand the basic reasons for the discord between the Allies which surfaced less than two weeks after the Yalta communiqué.

We have seen many alliances fall apart after victory. Rarer are the cases in which, agreements having hardly been signed, it is discovered that a basic disagreement wins out over the assumed understanding. Rarer still are those in which, through crises and negotiations and new crises

---

1. Maxim Maximovich Litvinov (1876–1951) had been a militant Bolshevik since 1898; commissioner for foreign affairs 1930–1939; and ambassador in Washington 1941–1943. In a conversation with the ambassador of the United States on May 25, 1946, Litvinov said, "All we can hope for today is an armed truce which will last long." Cf. J. Laloy, "Les avertissements de Litvinov," in *L'historien et les relations internationales* (Geneva: I.U.H.E.I, 1981), 325–326.

followed by new discussions, the disagreement persists for forty years without an end in sight. The cycle which originated in the Crimea is not over today.

The Three Great Powers

The leaders of this strange alliance were three men whose names are impressive, but who were, after all, only men.

Winston Spencer Churchill, the oldest of the three (he was seventy-one years old in 1945) reveals enough of himself in his memoirs to make a lengthy portrait unnecessary. Capricious, hotheaded, an improviser, and frequently intolerable; but also far-sighted, tenacious, and sensitive; capable simultaneously of brutality, of generosity, and of humor, not to say puerility, he was doubtless the first to grasp the fact that the end of hostilities would not mean the return of peace.

Franklin D. Roosevelt, according to all who knew him, remains elusive: both a sincere idealist and a political realist;[2] frequently superficial and yet a man of convictions; arousing crowds with his speeches, but disappointing his interlocutor by the incoherence of his remarks. He was one of the artisans of the victory of 1945, but not without some responsibility for the disappointments that followed; the president, who died when he was sixty-three, left no memoirs through which to fathom his secret. Although he was capable of much improvisation, superficial judgment, and carelessness, one must nevertheless recognize that as early as June 1940 he understood what was at stake, that as early as March 1941 he converted his country into "the arsenal

---

2. "I dream dreams but am, at the same time, an intensely practical person." Letter to Marshal Smuts, November 24, 1942, quoted by J. M. Burns, *Roosevelt, the Soldier of Freedom* (New York: Harcourt Brace Jovanovich, 1970), 609.

of democracy," and that as early as Pearl Harbor he firmly upheld the principle of Atlantic priority—"Atlantic first." But while he was clear-sighted on the nature of the enemy, he was grossly mistaken on that of his eastern ally.

Joseph V. Stalin, once admired by many people, is today disparaged, not to say held in contempt. In 1944, General de Gaulle saw in him a *"charme ténébreux"* (gloomy charm). Churchill and Roosevelt also felt something of that charm. (As he was leaving a session at Potsdam, Churchill said, "I like that man."[3]) Those who met him during and after the war were more conscious of what his daughter Svetlana terms "the emptiness he had created within himself": he was a man who had attained the peak of power by the most perverse methods and, not having found there what he expected, was a totally disenchanted man. "I no longer trust anyone," said he one day in Khrushchev's presence, "not even myself!"[4] He was a man who continued, by ferocity and guile, to accumulate power, land, influence, and domination, and who in the depths of his subconscious had a foreboding of emptiness, of horror: all to what purpose! "Stalin," Bukharin[5] said during a visit to Paris in 1936, "is wretched because he cannot convince everyone, not even himself, that he is greater than everyone else . . . his wretchedness compels him to take revenge on people, all people . . . he will devour us."[6] As insensitive

3. A. Eden, *The Reckoning* (Boston: Houghton Mifflin Co., 1965), 632.

4. N. S. Khrushchev, *Khrushchev Remembers,* ed. and tr. Strobe Talbot (Boston: Little, Brown & Co., 1970), 244.

5. Nicolas Ivanovich Bukharin (1888–1938), who was "the darling child of the Party," according to Lenin, and editor-in-chief of *Pravda* in 1917, opposed Stalin after Lenin's death, advocated "proletarian humanism," and was tried and condemned to death in 1938; he was officially rehabilitated fifty years later, in 1988.

6. Cf. Stephen F. Cohen, *Bukharin and the Bolshevik Revolution* (New York: Vintage Books, 1971), 365, and L. Dan, "Bukharin o Staline," *Novyi Journal,* no. 75 (1964): 181–182.

to overtures as to threats, he was imbued with distrust and suspicion. "A monster of guile," said a French diplomat who had long observed him,[7] "a monster of rancor!" Nothing but the world! Nothing but nothing! He was desiccated, disgusted, and unceasingly active, employing harsh measures and deceit, but without ever obtaining the satisfaction he awaited. Omnipotent, but a captive of this omnipotence, he had no instruments other than force and guile at the service of his rancor. How could anyone have a meeting of minds with him?[8]

Europe Out of the Game

Those who criticize the Yalta agreements as disastrous for Europe leave out of account a whole segment of reality: Europe, as much the hearth of civilization and culture as of rivalry and war; that Europe, weakened since 1919, collapsed in June 1940. After the fall of France, the Continent was handed over to Hitler. When he attacked the USSR, Europe was caught up in what soon became a race toward the abyss.

From June 1941 on, no one had any control over events any more, Hitler was an outlaw, and Europe lay underfoot. The conflict was wholly out of control. The final outcome left was the destruction of the enemy. The Allies were thus welded to each other. But as allies in spite of themselves in an inexpiable conflict, they had no common goals, few means of influencing each other, and few facili-

7. Jean Payart was stationed in Moscow for almost ten years (1930–1940), later high commissioner in Austria, ambassador of France, etc.

8. We do not go into the question here of whether Stalin was "paranoid" or not. B. Souvarine, in the postface of his 1935 book, which was republished, *Staline* (Paris Editions Champ Libre, 1977, 581–582), asserts this as a certainty: In his physical appearance Stalin had something of a monster about him, not of a psychopathic case. It is true that there isn't much difference between them.

ties through which to reconcile their views. To reproach
them for not having done better is to forget that prior to
Hitler's fall, they didn't have much choice. It is also to
forget, when those criticisms are aired in France, that many
of the misfortunes of Europe during and since the war were
due to the French defeat. After June 1940, the Continent
had been swept bare. It is true that the governments-in-
exile, the resistance movements, attempted to foresee the
future. To prepare for it was another matter. Short of an
alliance united in a common undertaking, the shape of the
future Europe depended above all on the outcome of the
fighting, of the line on which the Allies would meet, some
of them landing in the western part of the Continent, the
others driving toward that same west.

Nothing reveals this state of affairs better than the
edict of "unconditional surrender" issued by Roosevelt in
Casablanca in January 1943. The common goal could only
be expressed in negative terms. No one knew what would
happen afterward. However, in the three capitals, thought
was being given to the future peace.

Plans for the Postwar Period

The preliminary work undertaken in Washington and
London with the postwar years in mind is well known. One
can form an idea of the plans for the future developed in
Moscow through the conversations, negotiations, and acts
of the Soviet leaders between 1941 and 1945.

Roosevelt's principal interest lay in the future relations
with the Soviet Union. He took a very detached view of
these. During most of the war, the American leaders
thought that the major postwar risk was a conflict of interests of the traditional kind between Great Britain and the
Soviet Union. In order to avoid this, Roosevelt tried to
establish special relations between the United States and

the Soviet Union, between Stalin and himself. The future of Europe was not his major concern; he was even less concerned with the future of central and eastern Europe. When he visited Washington in March 1943, Anthony Eden noted, not without surprise, that when it was a matter of the Baltic countries or of the frontier between Poland and the USSR, the president was prepared to compromise on the liberal principles of the Atlantic Charter, the document he had signed with Churchill in August 1941.[9]

According to Roosevelt, future peace was to be preserved by an international organization consisting of an assembly as well as various councils or committees, but in fact directed by the three victors (plus China) and responsible for international security, hence for the police. There was to be no going back to the League of Nations and its ineffectualness! The enemies, after their defeat, would remain disarmed; the other countries would no longer need large forces. Peace would be secured under the control of the Directorate of the Four (plus, possibly, France). This peace would be reinforced to the extent that colonies, mandated territories, or territories under control, would gradually acquire their independence, thanks to a system of international supervision (trusteeship). Finally, international economic relations would be organized under a series of agreements, so as to achieve a system of exchanges as little restrictive as possible. Behind these very broad views, one detects the desire not to repeat the Wilson experience and hence to organize international relations on a new basis: permanent institutions, created, if possible, prior to the cessation of hostilities; a definitive involvement by the United States in international political action; and maintenance of good relations between the victors chiefly responsible for the future, especially the United States and the

9. Eden, *The Reckoning*, 432.

USSR. In this program, idealism and pragmatism inevitably became entangled. The missing element was an understanding of the nature and intentions of the great ally to the east.

The Soviet Union had, from the start, its own views on Germany. These views were, if one may so call them, "dialectical": first annihilate Hitler, Hitlerism, and all that goes with it (which implied the overturning of the economic and social structures of the vanquished country) and next, bring about the rebirth of a new Germany,[10] and thus form the cadres of the future Germany. As early as 1942, the German communists who had fled to the USSR addressed themselves to this task under the direction of Walter Ulbricht; they were joined, in 1943, by the Free Germany Committee and the League of German Officers, established in the USSR after the German surrender at Stalingrad.[11]

Between Germany and the USSR, the eastern countries, in particular Poland, constituted a screen between 1919 and 1939. After the victory, the security requirements of the USSR would have to be met. In the whole of central or eastern Europe, regroupings of a federal character would be prohibited as being inspired by the idea of a *cordon sanitaire* isolating the USSR. In the west, when General de Gaulle invoked, in a speech in March 1944, the project of a "western entity," he was sternly called to order by Moscow: no "western bloc" either!

The picture which emerged was of a Europe over which the USSR—freed of all *cordons sanitaires,* federations, and other obstacles—would, through the eastern countries and Poland in particular, play a preponderant role: directly

10. "History teaches us that Hitlers come and go, but that the German people, the German State, remain." Stalin, "Order of the Day, February 23, 1942," in *Vnechnaïa Politika SSSR,* vol. 1 (Moscow, 1946), 58.

11. W. Leonhard, *Die Revolution entlässt ihre Kinder* (Cologne: Kiepenheuer & Witsch, 1955), esp. Chapts. 6 and 7.

over a defeated Germany and indirectly beyond, i.e., over
France and the countries bordering on the Atlantic. "What
frightens me, however," wrote the U.S. Ambassador to
Moscow Averell Harriman in September 1944,

> is that when a country starts extending its influence
> by strong arm methods beyond its borders under
> the guise of security, it is difficult to see where a
> line can be drawn. Once the policy is accepted that
> the Soviet Union has a right to penetrate her
> immediate neighbors for security reasons,
> penetration of the next immediate neighbors
> becomes, at a certain point, equally logical.[12]

Rare at this time were those who were aware of the
problem so defined.[13]

People in London were more aware of European realities than people in Washington and thus more conscious of
the weight the USSR would be bringing to bear on Europe.
London was the capital of the governments-in-exile. Some
of these, specifically those of Poland and Czechoslovakia,
envisaged a regrouping of a federal character as early as
1940.

The departments of the Foreign Office drafted various proposals concerning postwar Europe. That which
emerged in 1942–1943 foresaw a restored France in the
west as a pillar of Western security against Germany; in the
center, a Germany reduced in size, but neither divided nor
carved up, in process of reintegration into the civilized
community;[14] to the east and southeast, various federal

12. *Foreign Relations of the United States,* vol. 4 (U.S. Government Printing
Office, Washington, D.C. 1944), 993.

13. An exception is the memorandum drafted by C. Bohlen, member of the
American delegation, after the Tehran Conference (see Chapt. 3, 40–42).

14. In September 1943, Anthony Eden wrote that "the only policy holding
out any real hope for the future is one which, while taking all necessary safe-

arrangements, for example, between Poland and Czecho-slovakia, between Yugoslavia and Greece. The idea was to create two zones of surveillance over the future Germany: one in which France, backed by Great Britain, would play an important role; the other in which the federations would rely on the support of the Soviet Union without being dom-inated by it. One sees in the background the idea of inter-posing between the USSR and Germany not a *cordon sani-taire* but a middle zone permitting the creation of a certain equilibrium among the various states, from the largest to the smallest.

Thus, there were important divergences between the Three Allies. This is not surprising. The functioning of the alliance of the Three was rendered difficult by the fact that the British and the Americans had at their disposal efficient institutions for reducing their differences—a common tongue and close relations between the president and the prime minister—whereas with the ally to the east, there was nothing—neither institutions nor language nor sentiments.

Two Alliances in One

One notes that for the entire duration of the war, both deep solidarity and profound divergences persisted be-tween London and Washington, not only in regard to long-term objectives and conditions for the return to peace, but also to the military operations ahead, and to strategy.

It is true that Roosevelt, upheld, not to say guided, by General Marshall, from the start gave priority to Europe, which after the disaster of Pearl Harbor was by no means self-evident. But how was this priority to be implemented?

---

guards, aims ultimately at the readmittance of a reformed Germany into the life of Europe," quoted in Llewellyn Woodward, *British Foreign Policy in the Second World War*, vol. 5 (London: HMS Office, 1976), 202.

The British, aware of the risks inherent in cross-channel operations (Hitler, at the peak of his power, had not dared risk them), managed, in July 1942, to impose the detour via the Mediterranean and North Africa. It was in Quebec, in September 1943, after Italy's collapse, that Churchill definitively committed himself to operation Overlord, or the landings in Normandy, but not without attempting to keep in reserve the possibility of diversions in the eastern Mediterranean.[15]

In the political realm, we have seen that the gulf was no less wide. Roosevelt feared being drawn after the war into the jungle of European rivalries. Churchill knew that in order to escape Soviet hegemony, Europe would need the support of the United States for a long time. However, he was not prepared to let the British empire disintegrate piece by piece. The longer the war lasted, the more Great Britain became conscious not only of the power, and thus of the role, but also of the weight of the United States in the alliance.

In the absence of an organization for policy coordination, these divergencies between the British and Americans could have become more serious but for the existence, in order to maintain the alliance, of three essential factors: the Atlantic Charter, the Combined Chiefs of Staff, and last, but not least, the personal ties between Churchill and Roosevelt.

People usually think of the Atlantic Charter as Metternich, in 1815, thought of the Holy Alliance: "An empty and resonant monument." This is partly true. But the charter included two important principles: "Their countries seek

---

15. Cf. Michael Howard, *The Mediterranean Strategy in the Second World War* (London, 1968). The author demonstrates that the object of these diversions was to exert pressure, now on the enemy's ocean flank, now on his Mediterranean flank; General Marshall was opposed to this on grounds of shortage of the indispensable physical resources required to implement these projects.

no aggrandizement, territorial or other," and "they desire to see no territorial changes that do not accord with the freely expressed wishes of the peoples concerned." For occupied Europe, the meaning of these principles was very clear. Stalin was aware of this. "I thought," he said in December 1941 to Anthony Eden, who was visiting Moscow, "that the Atlantic Charter was directed against those who are trying to establish world dominion. It now looks as though the charter were directed against the USSR."[16] The territories involved were those annexed by the USSR at the time of the German-Soviet entente. The charter was, therefore, not devoid of significance.

As for the Western alliance, it did not lack its structures. Churchill rushed to Washington in December 1941 where a mixed Anglo-American staff, the Combined Chiefs of Staff, was created. Its discussions were frequently very lively. But those discussions gave the governments the possibility of understanding each other in time and thus of reaching agreement if they wanted to. Along the same lines, mixed boards, or the Combined Boards, would function in Washington for the duration of the war, with the task of allocating to each of the two allies tonnage, raw materials, and so on.[17]

Neither the charter nor the chiefs of staff nor the Combined Boards would have sufficed without the personal relations between the two leaders. One only has to recall the effect of the manifold incompatibilities between de Gaulle and Roosevelt on Franco-American relations to attribute great importance to the bonds between the prime minister and the president. Certainly, under the increasing weight of his formidable ally, Churchill, reduced to the role of a brilliant second, often felt ill at ease. Instead of taking

16. Eden, *The Reckoning,* 343.

17. Cf. J. Monnet, *Mémoires* (Paris: Fayard, 1976), 209–212.

umbrage, he knew that by speaking directly to the president, he could make himself heard.

The Anglo-American alliance was certainly not idyllic. In particular, the relations of the Big Two with their allies of lesser weight were not always noted for their tact or delicacy. However, the reality was very different from the picture frequently drawn: two cronies, more or less cynical, more or less realistic, and disciples of Machiavelli rather than of Saint Louis. Let us see them as most men are, in between the two: while noting the realism of the one, nevertheless aware of the nobility of heart of the other.

With the ally to the east it was a different story.

We can start with a simple fact, so simple that it often passes unnoticed. On August 23, 1939, Stalin signed an agreement with Hitler which very rapidly brought him benefits, specifically territories. Less than two years later his accomplice leaped at his throat. After such a failure the one responsible for it should normally have resigned, or at least disappeared for a certain length of time. Stalin himself admitted as much at the end of the war: "A different people could have said to the government: 'You have failed to justify our expectations. Go away. We shall install another government!' "[18] In 1941 nothing of the sort occurred! The people, of course, remained silent. As for the party, it cannot make a mistake; therefore, Stalin did not make a mistake. Admittedly stupefied by the shock, he only pulled himself together one week later. When he finally spoke to the people on July 3, calling on them to resist, he nonetheless continued to defend his policy of the summer of 1939. How could he have admitted that between 1939 and 1941 he had completely gone astray? Indeed, he did not restrict himself to a nonaggression pact. On September 28, Molotov signed the "German-Soviet Boundary and Friendship Treaty" with Ribbentrop, which handed almost half of Po-

18. Stalin, "Speech of May 24, 1945," in *War Speeches* (London, 1976), 139.

land over to the USSR. As early as July 1941, Stalin laid claim to this territory, so wrongly acquired and so soon lost, from his alternative allies and, in the beginning, from Poland herself.

Thus was hatched the drama which poisoned relations between the Big Three during the entire war and beyond it. Whatever the realities of the ethnic situation on the borders of Poland and Russia, how could the Polish government-in-exile cede to an ally, *before the peace agreement,* 180,000 square kilometers, almost half the territory for which it was juridically and politically responsible? Of course "dialectics" furnish justification of any *fait accompli.* Besides, frontiers, and this one in particular, are not immutable. But can one ally impose them by force on another ally? The problem is not moral, but practical. How can normal relations, that is to say founded on reciprocity, be established with a government which, having joined the Western alliance against its own will, nevertheless intends to keep the territories which, yesterday, with the complicity of Hitler, it had wrenched from Poland, now its ally?

If the first maxim of natural law is Do not unto others that which you do not want them to do to you, the law of the Soviet leaders in 1941 was, rather, I do to others that which I would not tolerate their doing to me. One is an ally only by force of circumstances, and by this only.

From this time on, there was never really any confidence. Roosevelt and Churchill never felt completely sure that Stalin was not going to play one of his tricks on them. Stalin, whose suspiciousness was unequaled, could only believe that his Western partners, reversing the trick he had played on them in 1939, would make arrangements at the last moment with some German authority to rob him of the fruits of victory.

Whatever may have been the high and low points of the tripartite alliance formed in 1941, it contained within itself a vacuum impossible to fill: *No rule in common!*

2

A Difficult Ally

(1941–1942)

THIRTY MORE MONTHS were to elapse before Stalin met with his new allies. The secretary general, now prime minister and commander-in-chief, soon thereafter marshal and even generalissimo, never traveled; at least not beyond certain limits. Sometimes he invoked his official duties, sometimes medical advice. But if one looks for a factor common to the three cities which were hosts to the Big Three: Tehran in 1943, Yalta and Potsdam in 1945, one notes in each case the presence of the Soviet armed forces, and thus of the necessary security apparatus. The reason behind this was doubtless the refusal to entrust even a particle of the security function to foreign services, whoever they might be.

In this first period of the alliance, contacts took the form of messages or messengers (Hopkins, personal adviser to Roosevelt in Moscow in July and September 1941; Eden in Moscow in December 1941, and in Washington in March 1943; Molotov in London and Washington in May–June 1942; not to mention Churchill, who went to America several times and, for more thankless tasks, to Moscow in August 1942 and October 1944). Contacts, conversation, and correspondence dealt essentially with two areas: to the west, the "second front" and to the east, Poland. The USSR demanded military assistance in Europe as soon as possible, not to say at once; at the same time it brought to bear heavy exactions on Poland and her government-in-exile. A curious situation! Of the three powers, the one most threatened also showed itself to be the least forthcoming.

The "Second Front"

As soon as he had collected his wits, Stalin, both in his public speeches and in his messages to his unexpected allies called for massive landings on the Continent.[1] This demand was easy to understand because his country, and with it the regime, seemed to be on the verge of collapse. The demand caused some raising of eyebrows among those who remembered that in May–June 1940, the French and British had deeply felt the absence of a "second front" to the east.[2] A demand frequently repeated in 1942 when, in the Pacific, the Americans were carrying the brunt of a

1. In April 1941, speaking to Matsuoka, minister of foreign affairs of Japan, with whom he had just signed a neutrality agreement, Stalin said, "Now that Japan and Russia have fixed their problems, Japan can straighten out the Far East; Russia and Germany will handle Europe. Later together all of them will deal with America." Cf. J. M. Burns, *Roosevelt, the Soldier of Freedom* (New York: Harcourt Brace Jovanovich, 1970), 95.

In the same spirit, Stalin said to his daughter, shortly after the war, "Well, together with the Germans we would have been invincible!" (S. Alliluyeva, *Only One Year*, New York, 1969, 392).

2. In May–June 1940, France and Great Britain urgently sent their ambassadors to Moscow to ask the USSR to help them avoid catastrophe in the west. The collapse of France relieved Stalin of the necessity of replying to this initiative. Cf. G. Ross, *The Foreign Office and the Kremlin*, Cambridge University Press, 1984, 7; and J. B. Duroselle, *L'abîme (1939–1945)*, Paris: Imprimerie Nationale, 1982, 73–74.

second front which had, among other things, the effect of
diverting Japan from any thrust against Soviet Siberia.

Stalin's insistence can be explained in several ways.

The first, and most obvious, reason was the extreme
danger which threatened not merely the country but the
regime, "Lenin's heritage," in other words, Stalin in person. In September 1941, did he not go so far as to suggest
to the British that they send thirty divisions to the eastern
front in order to check the German advance?[3] Thirty divisions! With their equipment and the lines of communication passing around South Africa! Isn't this evidence of his
state of utter confusion? Better than anyone, since he was
the one responsible for them, he knew the horrors of fren-
zied industrialization, of the collectivization of land, and of
the "dekulakization," the terrible years of the thirties. In
August 1942, telling Churchill of the struggle against the
kulaks, the prosperous peasants, he said, "It was worse than
the present war."[4] And to Harriman, in September 1941,
"the Russian people are fighting, as they always have, 'for
their homeland, not for us.' "[5] Up until autumn 1942, Stalin attacked the "traitors," the "deserters," the "spreaders
of false news," and the *intelligentiki,* the intellectual deca-
dents, in his public speeches.

He deemed it necessary to recall several times that the
"national socialists" had nothing to do with socialism.
They were invaders and pillagers. If he took the trouble to
say this, it was doubtless because some people were asking
themselves, wouldn't a different "socialism" be, all things

3. Stalin to Churchill, September 13, 1941, in *Sovetsko-Angliskie Otnocheniia
(1941–1945),* vol. 1 (Moscow, 1983), 118.

4. W. Churchill, *The Second World War,* vol. 4, *The Hinge of Fate* (Boston:
Houghton Mifflin, 1950), 498.

5. A. Harriman and E. Abel, *Special Envoy to Churchill and Stalin, 1941–1946*
(New York: Random House, 1975), 521.

considered, less bad than Stalin's? In October 1941, according to the few remaining foreigners in Moscow, numerous signs of disaffection were evident, the regime seemed close to the last gasp.[6]

Thus the repeated public clamor for the second front can easily be explained by the necessity of reassuring the troops and consolidating the rear (without overlooking other more effective methods). But it also stemmed from other calculations, which were aimed at the Allies.

For the long term, one must avoid having the Western forces standing there at attention. Stalin, should he recall his thoughts during the summer of 1939, had every reason to fear that his new allies, rather than committing themselves fully, would confine themselves to encouraging him by furnishing arms and materials and would emerge from the war in the position he had foreseen for himself: that of arbiter between the exhausted enemies. One finds a hint of these thoughts and suspicions in Stalin's comments about France: "the French contribution at the present time to military operations on the Western Front was very small" and "in 1940 they had not fought at all."[7] He harbored a grudge against France for having, by her incapacity, caused the failure of the plan he had in mind in the spring of 1939. His allies must not be allowed to play the same trick on him, albeit in a different way.

For the immediate future, it was a matter of exerting

---

6. According to the Turkish ambassador in Moscow, "the fall of Smolensk [July 16, 1941] had made a deep impression in Moscow, people were beginning to criticize the government openly, they had the impression that the war was lost." Cf. Llewellyn Woodward, *British Foreign Policy in the Second World War*, vol. 2 (London: HMS Office, 1976), 19, and A. Wenger, *Rome and Moscow 1900–1950* (Paris, 1987), 10–11.

7. Conversation between Stalin and Roosevelt at Yalta, February 4, 1945, in *Foreign Relations of the USA, The Conferences of Malta and Yalta* (Washington, D.C.: U.S. Government Printing Office, 1955), 572.

pressure on the Allies so as to obtain material assistance from them as rapidly as possible.[8] Finally, as regards the subsequent period, so long as the Allies had not landed they would have a bad conscience which Stalin could exploit to gain political advantages for the postwar period. Hence his insistence was understandable. One also understands the interest the Allies would have had in intervening rapidly and massively. Not only would they have brought relief to the USSR, but they could have thrust deeply into the Continent, thereby forming a counterweight to Soviet military power. Why didn't they?

We know that until July 1942, the Americans were insisting on landing on the Continent. The British, involved in various operations in Africa, were more keenly conscious of the difficulties of the enterprise. The compromise solution was the landings in North Africa in the fall of 1942, Roosevelt not finding acceptable the prospect of keeping his forces inactive one whole year on the Atlantic front. Many writers assert that had one accepted the sacrifice of many lives, it would have been possible to invade the European continent from the west as early as 1942. But, in order to win a victory, is it enough to sacrifice the lives of soldiers? Does one not run the risk of the double disappointment of heavy losses and of failure? Without claiming to settle the point, one may nevertheless take into account the views of two experts.

> The most effective help, if indeed it could have been given, would have been the "Second Front" for which there was such an insistent demand [from Moscow]—a massive landing on the coast of France; and under the insistent pressure of the Prime

---

8. Under Lend-Lease the United States was to supply the USSR with arms and various material, including civilian equipment, equivalent in value to almost $10 billion (see Chapt. 6, 91).

Minister the Chiefs of Staff examined ways and means by which this could be done. But they could find no escape from their dilemma; they did not in 1941 or 1942 have the resources for a sufficiently massive landing to affect the issue in the Soviet Union, while a landing on the only scale that they could manage could be contained, and probably destroyed by the German forces in western Europe without a man, a tank, a gun, or an aircraft being moved from the Russian front. American forces might have made such a landing possible in 1943; but to allow a full year to pass without any sizeable element of the Axis forces being engaged in the west at all was regarded as domestically unaccept-able, strategically unsound, and imposing an unacceptable strain on the resources and loyalty of the Soviet Union. Hence the decision taken in summer 1942 to concentrate on the Mediterranean, even though this was known to render any "Second Front" impracticable until 1944.[9]

These views were endorsed by General Marshall, one of the foremost supporters of a landing in Europe, who nevertheless stated, "The difference between a river cross-ing, however wide, and a landing from the ocean is that the failure of a river crossing is a reverse while the failure of a landing operation is a catastrophe."[10]

One is therefore inclined to believe that the public and repeated call for the second front is to be explained not only by the instinctive need of being backed up in a dra-matic crisis, but also by more complex and longer term

9. M. Howard, "Strategy and Politics in World War II: The British Case," in *Politics and Strategy in the 2nd World War* (Kansas State University, 1976), 37.

10. R. Sherwood, *Roosevelt and Hopkins* (New York: Harper and Brothers, 1948), 783.

political considerations. This was made clear by the debate over Poland in 1941–1942.

Poland

As we have seen above,[11] the claims of the USSR concerning Poland were put forward as early as the first days of July 1941. It was due only to pressure by the British government that General Sikorski agreed to sign an agreement with the USSR on July 30, even though the total opposition between the signatories over the line of the frontier between the two countries had not been overcome.

When Anthony Eden went to Moscow in December 1941 to negotiate what was to become, in May 1942, the Anglo-Soviet Alliance, Stalin laid down a precondition: Does Great Britain recognize, or not, the frontiers of her ally as they existed on June 22, 1941, that is, in Poland, the Ribbentrop-Molotov line? It was a crucial moment, perhaps a missed opportunity. In fact, Eden took no position. He merely said that the British cabinet had promised the United States government not to commit itself on territorial issues prior to the peace conference. This was true. After a few fairly sharp exchanges, Stalin refused to conclude an alliance which did not include a protocol concerning specific problems, especially that of the frontiers of the USSR. The British hesitated up to the spring of 1942. Finally, they declared themselves ready to agree to Stalin's demands. In May, Molotov was in London. Roosevelt, opposed to all bilateral agreements prior to the peace conference, invited Molotov to Washington in order to tell him about a "big military operation" in 1942, whereupon Molotov gave up on the Anglo-Soviet protocol on the frontier, signed the treaty of alliance with Great Britain as it stood,

11. See Chapt. 1, 16–17.

and obtained, more or less in return, a half-promise of a second front, a half-promise (because the text is ambiguous[12]) which was to be only partially kept by the landings in North Africa in November 1942. As a result, the British and Americans, unable to satisfy Stalin on the second front tended to accept the frontier which the latter wished to impose on Poland.

What would have happened if, in reply to Stalin's first request, Eden had at once replied in substance: "You cannot demand of Sikorski that he should accept a frontier you have obtained from Hitler. On the other hand one could envisage at the end of the war a frontier settled amicably with the Polish government, which would be neither that of 1921 nor that of 1939. Along those lines we will back you up. Let us not go any further for the time being. With patience, we shall perhaps arrive at an agreement acceptable to both parties. Your present position does not permit this. We cannot go along with it as it is."

Had he refused, Stalin would have shown himself in his true colors, which, in 1941, would have had certain disadvantages for him. Had he accepted, he would no doubt have had to give up Lvov and part of Galicia, which he seemed to have contemplated doing at the end of 1941.[13] In return, he might have reestablished a reasonable relationship with Poland, perhaps even eventually wiping the slate clean. One might have reached that provisional "line

12. "American-Soviet communiqué, June 12, 1942: In the course of the conversations, full understanding was reached with regard to the urgent tasks of creating a second front in Europe in 1942." H. Feis, *Churchill, Roosevelt, Stalin* (Princeton, N.J.: Princeton University Press, 1957), 67.

13. Cf. V. Mastny, *Russia's Road to the Cold War* (New York: Columbia University Press, 1979), 54. Sikorski's memorandum of his conversation with Stalin said, "He told me of Soviet goodwill in this direction, and of the assistance which Russia was ready to give us in our disputes with the Ukrainians in the matter of the Polish city of Lvov." *Documents on Polish-Soviet Relations*, vol. 1 (London, 1960), 264–265.

of demarcation" which the Polish government was to propose in 1944 and which Stalin at once rejected because it
was "provisional."

For lack of adequate clarification, each side held to its
position. A serious dispute separated the Soviets from the
Poles, a dispute which grew steadily worse, and whose end
result was to be the enslavement of Poland.[14] This was
difficult to avoid. One might perhaps have succeeded in
working out a form of limited, yet real, independence between independence and enslavement. This was very un-
likely. In the event of success, it would have changed the
face of Europe.

We must therefore ask ourselves why Stalin, who knew
that he would need Poland after the war, put forward a
condition which rendered an understanding with the Polish
government impossible.

A first answer is that he could not back down because
he did not believe in good feelings such as would be
aroused in his partners by an act of generosity on his part.
Stalin would, if so, have been less a prisoner of his policy
than of his sense of absolute realism. This answer contains
a substantial element of truth. But the example of Finland
after the war shows that, at least in one case (involving a
defeated enemy, not an ally), Stalin was able to moderate
his position. We must therefore look further for an explanation.

In 1941–1942, no one knew what would become of
Germany after the war. On whom could Stalin count in
order to keep her under observation? The Americans
would not stay on forever. The British and the French

14. In a resolution adopted in Warsaw in April 1945 by a popular meeting,
we find the following sentence: "The Polish people realize that their *independence
depends* on friendship with the Soviet Union," *Izvestia*, April 24, 1945, quoted by
A. A. Gromyko and B. N. Ponomarev, *Istoriia Vnechinei polititiki SSSR*, vol. 1
(Nauka, Moscow, 1976), 486, emphasis added by Jean Laloy.

could not be counted upon. The USSR could count only on itself. It must therefore have direct access to Germany. This access, this "corridor," as Stalin said repeatedly, was Poland. After what occurred between 1939 and 1941 in the Polish territories annexed by the USSR (massive deportations, executions, arrests, and persecutions), it would be difficult to count on her friendship. She must therefore be constrained. Hence no concessions, no compromises.

According to this interpretation, we start with the idea that in eastern Europe the policy of the USSR was less that of a *defensive glacis,* an idea accepted by most historians, than that of an *access corridor to Germany.* In the background: "Never that again!" Never again be cut off from Germany, the only real danger for the USSR after the war, should she rise again from her ashes; but also, if subjugated, an excellent springboard for any influence the USSR might exercise as far as possible toward the west of the Continent. Under these conditions, the frontier of September 28, 1939, was, for Stalin, the touchstone of "friendship" between Poland and the USSR. The government which accepted would be friendly. Why? Because the government which accepted it would sever itself from the nation, and be dependent on the (good) will of the USSR. The only friends were those who were submissive.

Here we are at the root not only of wartime difficulties, but of the postwar up until today. If this was not clearly grasped at the time, it was because the popularity of the Soviet ally during the war was very great, whereas the Polish government-in-exile never succeeded in making itself properly heard. For many people in the west, Poland was still the Poland of before 1939: unrealistic, romantic, and irresponsible.

Seen from this angle, the question of the frontier between Poland and the USSR appeared relatively minor. If Stalin were given satisfaction, it was thought that there would be a good chance of seeing normal relations develop between the two countries. Why should Poland hang on to the Pripet marshes when it could acquire rich land and modern industrial equipment in the west?

By basing itself on the pragmatic realism of traditional diplomacy, London misread the nature of the problem, its *ethical* dimension, a dimension *politically* essential. The same applied to Roosevelt for roughly the same reasons. And also, it would seem, to General de Gaulle if, as the Soviet memorandum of a conversation with the ambassador of the USSR reported, the general did in fact say in the spring of 1943 that "if he were to come to power, France would without any doubt support Russia in favor of a frontier in the spirit of the Curzon line."[15]

The real problem was how to establish a territorial status between the USSR and Poland that was acceptable to both and assured the latter the indispensable degree of independence. Indispensable not only for Poland, but for peace in Europe in conformity with what used to be called in the nineteenth century the "Public Law of Europe." Churchill was perhaps to become aware of this in 1944 and doubtless General de Gaulle as well, after his visit to Moscow in December of the same year. And Roosevelt asked himself in April 1945, a few days before his death, whether Stalin had not made a fool of him.

Did Stalin hoodwink his allies? Placed in a position of inferiority by the German offensive (he needed their help during the war and their understanding after the war for the policy he intended to carry out in Europe and Asia), he

15. "Meeting between de Gaulle and Bogomolov, London, May 11, 1943," in *Sovetsko-Frantsuzskie Otnocheniia (1941–1945)*, vol. 1 (Moscow, 1983), 176–178. The Curzon line is the same one proposed by Lord Curzon in 1919 as Poland's frontier. Its course is not identical with that of the frontier of 1939, but runs very close to it.

exploited the lack of a second front in Europe until 1944 in order to get his allies to go along with his major demands on Poland, eastern Europe, and, in the center, Germany. He never ceased lending currency to the idea that in the absence of a second front he would not be able to continue alone to contain the enemy's offensives. This is what Molotov led Roosevelt to understand in May 1942. This was doubtless the reason behind the unofficial German-Soviet contacts in Stockholm in 1943.[16] The thought occurs to one that, for Stalin, it was less a matter of a separate peace than a maneuver designed to foster reservations among his allies, especially toward their ally Poland. Typical in this respect was Churchill's behavior in May 1942 when he was prepared to recognize the frontier which Stalin wanted to impose on Poland. Similarly, in January 1943, Roosevelt hesitated to intervene with Stalin concerning the measures taken against the Poles who were deported in 1939 from the territories that were annexed by the USSR and who, in 1943, found themselves to be Soviet citizens against their will.[17]

Stalin only hoodwinked his allies insofar as they did not thwart his maneuvers by raising the tone of the debate in such a way as to show themselves to be Allies, of course, but nevertheless standing fast on the basic principles without which there can be neither understanding nor peace.

16. Cf. Jan Ciechanowski, *Defeat into Victory* (New York: Doubleday and Co., 1947), Chapt. 16, 138–146.

17. Ibid.

3

From Casablanca to Tehran

(1943)

In 1943, THE HORIZON grew brighter. No more victories for Hitler!

After the catastrophe of Stalingrad in January, the Wehrmacht was unable to recapture the offensive in the region of Kursk in May. It retreated in disorder under the weight of the Soviet counteroffensive, considered today by the USSR to have been the real turning point of the war in Europe.

In the Pacific, after the battle of Midway in 1942 and especially of Guadalcanal, which ended in February 1943, the Japanese advance was halted. In the Mediterranean, the German-Italian forces were chased out of North Africa in May. Italy surrendered on September 3. In the Atlantic, from the spring of 1943 on, the Allies regained the upper hand, and German submarines were being efficiently hunted down.

Churchill and Roosevelt met in Casablanca from January 14 to 23 in order to coordinate their strategic plans (and to attempt, after the North African landings, to settle their relations with the Free French). Stalin, who had been invited, did not find it possible to attend. In April, he broke relations with the Polish government in London over the Katyn affair. In July, he protested against a further postponement of the Normandy landings. But in September, following Italy's surrender, the necessity of consultation won the day. The outcome of the conferences in Moscow in October, and Tehran in December, brought Stalin perhaps more from his allies than he had expected, particularly in regard to the two key countries, Poland and Germany.

"Unconditional Surrender"

At Anfa, near Casablanca, the tasks of the president and the prime minister were to define their strategic plans for the year 1943. Following closely argued discussions between the military authorities, it was decided to pursue operations in the Mediterranean, i.e., to invade Sicily after the African campaign. The landings in France, still called for by the Soviets, were postponed to the following year, always for the same reason: the war being waged over two oceans was absorbing all the available means of transportation; the quantity of available landing barges was far from adequate. If, after Sicily, Italy could be knocked out of the war, the Germans would have to defend themselves on three fronts. However these arguments were not persuasive to Stalin.

For public opinion, the Casablanca Conference was above all concerned with the "unconditional surrender" of the enemy. Roosevelt announced this to the press on January 24 in Churchill's presence:

> Peace can come to the world only by the total
> elimination of German and Japanese war power. . . .
> The elimination of German, Japanese, and Italian
> war power means the unconditional surrender of
> Germany, Italy, and Japan. . . . It does not mean

the destruction of the population of Germany, Italy, or Japan, but it does mean the destruction of the philosophies of those countries which are based on conquest and the subjugation of other people.[1]

Churchill, while taken by surprise, approved. He had already discussed the subject with the president, but was not at all expecting a public statement broadcast worldwide.

According to Roosevelt, this idea occurred to him suddenly. But during the conference, he had papers before him, which implies a certain amount of preparation. In fact, this announcement was to be explained by tactical considerations. In order not to find himself at the end of the fighting in the same position as Wilson in 1918–1919—tugged between the Allies looking for guarantees and the losers who, for their part, sheltered behind the principles proclaimed by Wilson—the president wanted in the shorter run to put an end to the criticism aroused in Algiers at the time of the landings by the agreements concluded with Darlan, "the provisional expedient." No compromise would be made with the enemy. Finally, he wanted to reassure the ally to the east. But there were deeper motives: unconditional surrender was logical in a conflict whose object was to destroy the Hitlerian regime—to destroy it totally—hence, there could be no discussion with it. The postwar plans prepared in 1943 by the State Department foresaw a long period for the reeducation of Germany: after the cessation of hostilities a year at least was to elapse before a new German government would be authorized.[2]

This said, was it appropriate to speak of unconditional surrender at this stage? Many people believe that by announcing this condition, Roosevelt contributed to prolong-

1. H. Feis, *Churchill, Roosevelt, Stalin* (Princeton, N.J.: Princeton University Press, 1957), 109.

2. See below, 38.

ing German resistance. This is likely. But from 1943 on, what favorable developments could the Germans expect?[3] It is true that the increasing number of people in Germany who understood that the war was lost found it harder and harder, after Roosevelt's statement, to organize a sufficient number of supporters to be able to act effectively. The venture was risky, as the failure of the July 1944 plot showed. It would perhaps have been less so had the conspirators been able to obtain some encouragement from London or Washington.[4] After all, in the summer of 1943 Stalin created the Free German Committee, a kind of training school for the managers of the future Germany. He did not hesitate to act in Poland without any regard for the views of his allies. Was it necessary to speak of unconditional surrender in 1943? Could one not, as Stalin had already been careful to do in 1942, have drawn a distinction between Hitler and the German people, thus encouraging the enemies of the regime to organize themselves with a view to taking action at the opportune moment? In any case, Roosevelt did not succeed in reassuring Stalin about the future. When the latter learned in July 1943 that the second front had been postponed to 1944, he recalled his ambassadors from London and Washington. In the meantime he had broken off relations with the Polish government-in-exile in London. Had Churchill and Roosevelt permitted some doubts to subsist on their intentions toward Germany, they might perhaps have been better heard in Moscow when it was necessary.

3. We know the phrase that was circulating in Germany in 1942: "Children, be glad we are at war! Peace will be still more terrible."

4. Cf. on this point the comments of Allen Dulles, European representative of the Office of Strategic Services, who regrets that nothing was done to encourage, at least by some public utterance, those who wanted to overthrow Hitler (Feis, *Churchill, Roosevelt, Stalin,* 356). In the same spirit, Charles E. Bohlen, *Witness to History* (New York: Norton and Co., 1973), 157–158.

The Katyn Affair

In April 1943, the German press and radio announced the discovery of the bodies of several thousand Polish officers in mass graves at Katyn near Smolensk. The Polish authorities had been searching since 1941 for these officers who had been taken prisoner by the Soviets in September 1939 and from whom nothing had been heard since April 1940. General Sikorski proposed a commission of inquiry under the auspices of the International Committee of the Red Cross (ICRC), whose seat is in Geneva. Arguing from the fact that the Germans had made a similar proposal, Moscow severed relations with the Polish government-in-exile, which it denounced as an accomplice of Hitler.[5]

The major Allies in the west had to react cautiously if they wished to avoid being drawn into the whirlwinds of this drama. In fact, there was no reaction. This enabled Stalin not only to extricate himself from the affair but also to profit from it. In Moscow, the Union of Polish Patriots, which was created in March 1943, increasingly assumed the character of a national committee. In 1942, the Polish army, recruited not without difficulty by General Anders from Polish prisoners freed by the USSR after June 22, 1941, left the USSR for the Near East, the Mediterranean, and Italy. In 1943, a Polish military unit was formed in the USSR under the orders of Colonel Berling. In Poland itself, a few Polish communist parachutists organized a Popular National Council and a Popular National Army, distinct from the army and from the National Council, which was under the government-in-exile. Thus a ditch was dug between the Three Allies, which would prove difficult to fill.

---

5. Cf. A. Kwiatkowska-Viatteau, *Katyn* (Brussels: Complexe, 1982) and J. Czapski, *Terre inhumaine* (Lausanne: L'Age d'homme, 1978). By the same author one may note the pamphlet published in Paris in 1945, *Souvenirs de Starobielsk* (collection Témoignages), which received little coverage at the time, where everything is revealed.

So, far from proving an embarrassment to Stalin, the revelation of the Katyn massacre furnished him with a pretext for taking a decisive step in regard to Poland; in 1943, he installed the principal elements of the future "Polish popular democracy": the clandestine Communist party in Poland, an embryo of a government and of a Polish army in the USSR. And it was at this moment that General Sikorski disappeared from the scene, a victim of a plane accident. He was replaced by the leader of the Peasant party, Stanislaw Mikolajczyk.

In the course of the summer, the fall of Mussolini and contacts between the new Italian government and the Western Allies distracted attention from events in the east and led to the Moscow and Tehran conferences.

The Surrender of Italy

When contacts were initiated in Lisbon, in August 1943, between the Italians and the Anglo-Americans, it seemed that unconditional surrender would be accompanied by a few promises for the future by virtue of the fact that Italy was preparing for "cobelligerence" on the side of the Allies. Moscow was being kept informed.

Suddenly, at the end of August, Stalin remembered a proposal Eden had made in July for an interallied commission to be charged with "directing and coordinating" all armistices in Europe.[6] He insisted that this commission be formed without delay. Thereupon hesitations arose, particularly in London. The political situation in Italy was complex and the war was not over; and on the strength of what was known of the methods of Soviet "cooperation," how

6. Cf. J. Laloy, "The Origins of the Division of Europe," *Review of Slavic Studies*, 54 (1982): 295–304; and especially H. Gladwyn Jebb, *The Memoirs of Lord Gladwyn* (London, 1972), Chaps. 9 and 10.

could the USSR be granted a right of veto over Allied policy in Italy? On the other hand, if one were to reject any Soviet presence in Italy, what would be the result for the Western powers in the eastern countries? To sum up: after thinking the matter over and exchanging telegrams, the Western Allies were prepared to accept the idea of the commission that Stalin had called for, but it was to be "consultative" in character, a means of exchanging views and not of decision making. The commander-in-chief must not be paralyzed, while the war lasted, by diplomats and their quibbles. In early September, Stalin agreed to this. But in the press and in the ministry headed by Molotov, calls continued for a commission with powers of decision. The dispute was resolved in the fall at the Moscow confer-ence attended by the three ministers of foreign affairs: the commission was to be consultative in character. It was to meet first in Algiers, then in Rome. Therefore, Anglo-American participation in the supervision of the armistices in eastern Europe would also be consultative in nature, that is to say, without much weight.

Should we see in this, as many people do, the first step toward the partition of Europe? For us, Italy, for you, the Balkans! Yes, if one does not take into account the principal cause of this partition: the difference between the regimes. No, if one recognizes that in Italy, which was soon to have a parliament, where the press was once again becoming pluralistic, and where there were numerous political par-ties, the Soviet Union had a variety of means of exerting influence, if not action, at its disposal (if only because of the presence of the Communist party, headed by Togliatti who had returned from Moscow); whereas in Romania, Bul-garia, or Hungary, the Anglo-Americans, in the absence of a free press and of a representative government could only recognize their own impotence. We too often forget that the partition of Europe already existed as early as 1944–1945 and that it was asymmetrical. The USSR dominated eastern and central Europe, but it also influenced the large Communist parties in the west, especially in France and Italy. Reciprocity was nonexistent: in the countries under Soviet control, the more or less liberal parties had been rapidly induced to join "fronts" dominated by the communists. "Two weights, two measures." Two zones: the one to the east congealed, the other to the west threatened with glaciation. The game was unequal. It still is today, even though hope has changed sides.

The Moscow Conference
(October 19–30, 1943)

Toward the end of August Stalin accepted the idea of a meeting with his two allies, to be preceded by a conference of foreign ministers. In Moscow they examined the future: the organization of world security after victory, European problems (Poland, Czechoslovakia, Germany, Italy, Yugoslavia, Greece, etc.), and the Far East.

The United States was represented by Cordell Hull, the old "white eagle" (he was seventy-two years old) whose two principal concerns were the postwar organization of a worldwide security system under the leadership of the "Great Powers" and the acceptance of China as a great power by the Three. As for the rest, that is to say Europe, he followed in silence the discussions between Molotov and Eden who, for want of support, was obliged to give ground. Hull did not have much trouble getting a declaration approved which provided for the creation of the body later known under the name of the United Nations. He succeeded in getting China accepted as a cosignatory of this declaration. Stalin personally told Hull that the USSR planned to intervene in the war against Japan when the time was ripe. Hull left reassured.

Anthony Eden had less reason to feel satisfied. The

British suggestions concerning the "common responsibility of the Three Powers in Europe" were accepted by the Soviets only under reserve of amendments which robbed them of any effectiveness; nor was any progress made on Poland or Yugoslavia. The partition of Europe, which was not yet complete, began to take shape, not only geographically, but also against the background of interallied discussions. The sole puny achievement was a consultative European commission (the European Advisory Commission, EAC) consisting of the three Allies (plus France beginning in November 1944), which was to meet in London and prepare the future according to the means at its disposal.

The Soviet Union had every reason to congratulate itself on this first meeting of the Three Powers: the United States adopted only a distant view of Europe and the British were unable to win acceptance of their ideas on the merits of groupings of a federal character between European countries, particularly in the east. Above all in two essential areas, Poland and Germany, the Soviet Union won great advantages for itself without any compensation. It severed relations in April with the Polish government without having to pay any price for this, and thus had no reason to change course. As for Germany, Hull gave Molotov an unofficial memorandum containing an essential provision for the future: after the surrender, there was to be no central German government, at least during an initial period estimated at six months or one year. No German Badoglio on the horizon! One understands why Molotov confided to Hull, with a beaming face, that Stalin found the American memorandum excellent, on condition that it should be considered "a minimum, and not a maximum." These prospects, which it was not very judicious to reveal so soon without counterparts, were confirmed and more than confirmed by the Tehran Conference (November 28–December 1, 1943).

The Tehran Meeting
(November 28–December 1, 1943)

Could it really be termed a conference? Four days of conversations among three men meeting for the first time without any preparation or agenda. What should we think of Roosevelt who, in order to avoid the insecurity of an inadequately guarded town, accepted Stalin's offer and went to stay in the Soviet Embassy? What should we think of the first tête-à-tête between Roosevelt and Stalin in which the president, in order to break the ice, indulged in a few jokes at Churchill's expense? Such remarks, while of little importance, must, given the Georgian's mental reservations, have served to increase his distrust.

From Tehran, Stalin and Molotov were able to draw three conclusions: they obtained a firm promise of landings on the French coast in 1944, and thus the quasi-certainty that there would be no Anglo-American military actions in the Balkans; they also received two major satisfactions, one on Poland and the other on Germany.

The situation in Poland was appalling: two rival resistance organizations, two armed forces, one fighting in Italy, the other being formed in the USSR; a National Committee was being prepared in the USSR to confront the government-in-exile in London—these constituted a heavy load for an alliance which was itself fragile. And on top of this, after dinner on November 29, Churchill made the suggestion to shift Poland westward: to the east, the Curzon line, which Stalin wanted, and to the west, no doubt, the Oder line. How could Stalin fail to feel more than ever convinced that the best policy was that of the *fait accompli*? No doubt Churchill hoped that in exchange for a territorial sacrifice, the Polish government-in-exile would be able to return to Warsaw. Isn't this what Beneš in his own way was attempting to do by proposing an assistance pact to the Soviet Union and by showing himself disposed to be very docile vis-à-vis Moscow? In Poland, things were different. Stalin would make the border he demanded the instrument enabling him to get rid of the Polish government, the one in London, which could not accept it. As for Beneš, he would return to Prague, but would immediately have to hand over to the USSR sub-Carpathian Ukraine; this was the eastern province of Czechoslovakia in 1919, where, as soon as the Soviet liberation forces had entered, national committees started calling for union with the Soviet Ukraine.

There was much talk about Germany at Tehran. Everyone raised the subject of its dismemberment. Roosevelt was thinking of five German states, Churchill of three. Stalin did not commit himself much, but he sensed more reservations in Churchill than in Roosevelt. Since Hull's October memorandum,[7] Stalin had reason to think that as concerned Germany, the Americans were not setting a trap for him. On the contrary! He saw the breach toward the west opening up before him: Moscow, Warsaw, Berlin. Congress, as Roosevelt had told Stalin, was opposed to the retention of American forces in Europe after the cessation of hostilities.[8] England would be weakened. France, in Stalin's view, no longer counted. France must lose her colonies, chief among which was Indochina, and offer her allies bases at Bizerte and Dakar. At least this was what he told Roosevelt.

What would remain of Europe as it was in 1939, after the victory?

There was one person who understood what was afoot. This was Charles E. Bohlen (first secretary at the embassy in Moscow), who was an expert in Soviet affairs and Roosevelt's interpreter and who, after returning from Tehran, gave Averell Harriman, U.S. ambassador in Moscow, the following memorandum.

7. See above, 38.

8. Feis, *Churchill, Roosevelt, Stalin,* 270.

The attitude of the Soviet Government toward each one of the questions listed in the attached document of course deserves detailed and special study. There are three, however, which are of particular interest since they form a pattern of Soviet views concerning post-war Europe. These three are:

1. Soviet opposition to federations.
2. Soviet determination to break up Germany.
3. The harsh attitude toward France.

To this should be added the Soviet preference for strong points or bases in Europe to be held by the three victorious powers as trustees. The most important indication of the Soviet concept of political organization after the war is found in the attitude toward France. The reasons advanced by Stalin for this attitude are not in themselves convincing and the facts in the French situation do not support the harshness of the treatment suggested. The real motive very probably lies elsewhere.

While this pattern obviously cannot be regarded as conclusive, it is sufficiently clear to afford a glimpse of the Soviet idea of post-war continental Europe. Germany is to be broken up and kept broken up. The states of eastern, southeastern and central Europe will not be permitted to group themselves into any federations or association. France is to be stripped of her colonies and strategic bases beyond her borders, and will not be permitted to maintain any appreciable military establishment. Poland and Italy will remain at approximately their present territorial size, but it is doubtful if either will be permitted to maintain any appreciable armed force.

The result would be that the Soviet Union would

be the only important military and political force on the continent of Europe. The rest of Europe would be reduced to military and political impotence.[9]

This memorandum appears to have had no effect. Harriman, according to what Bohlen writes about him in his memoirs, "had an enormous capacity for assessing the tactical nature of a problem. . . . But he did not take the indispensable step of relating his keen observations to the over-all Soviet ideological attitude toward the world and the capitalist nations."[10]

It was in the spring of 1945, after what may be termed the failure of Yalta, that Harriman became the advocate of a policy of resistance to the encroachments of the Soviet Union.[11] But there is today no doubt that these encroachments were already in Stalin's mind as early as 1943. Thanks to Bohlen, we also know that it was possible to detect them at the time, on condition of not being myopic.

9. *Foreign Relations of the United States, Cairo and Teheran* (Washington, D.C.: Government Printing Office, 1961), 845.

10. Bohlen, *Witness to History,* 127.

11. A. Harriman and E. Abel, *Special Envoy to Churchill and Stalin, 1941–1946* (New York: Random House, 1975), Chapts. 18–22.

4

From Teheran to Yalta: Europe in Ruins

(1944–1945)

IN A NORMAL ALLIANCE, in which each member argues his own viewpoint while also taking into account a certain degree of solidarity, 1944 could have been the year of understanding among the Allies.

In the east, before launching the offensive which in late July was to bring its forces before Warsaw, the Soviet Union obtained at the Tehran Conference, without having had to offer any concession, the assurances concerning its frontier with Poland for which it was asking its allies. Churchill was clear; Roosevelt let it be known that he had no objection to a transfer of Polish territory from east to west. On the western side, commitments were honored. As early as January 1944, Anthony Eden tried to persuade the Polish leaders to accept the "Curzon line." On February 22, before the Commons, Churchill expressed his support for the Soviet position on the frontier.

The Normandy landings in June opened up a new

phase of the war in Europe. "The armed forces of our allies," Stalin said, "have achieved an exploit without precedent in history in its scale and organization."[1] Thus one might have recorded progress on two fronts: the vise tightening on Germany and the alliance growing stronger proportionately to military success.

The reality was quite otherwise: in August 1944, with the support of the Allies, Paris in revolt was liberated. General de Gaulle marched down the Champs-Élysées surrounded by a huge crowd, which we shall see again on November 11, this time cheering de Gaulle and Churchill. Between August 1 and October 3, the uprising in Warsaw was annihilated for want of adequate assistance from the nearby Soviet forces. In the west there was liberation and popular jubilation. In the east, to use a lapidary phrase of Christian Fouchet in one of his reports to Paris: "liberation is terror."[2] How did this come about? We were up against the insoluble problem, not of relations between the USSR and Poland, but between the USSR and the rest of the world, in this case Poland.

The Polish-Soviet Frontier

On his return from Tehran, Churchill received the Polish leaders. The Minister of Foreign Affairs Tadeusz Romer, perhaps recalling Beneš at the time of Munich, implied that if the three major Allies were to recommend

1. Stalin, "Speech on the occasion of the 27th anniversary of the revolution, Moscow, November 6, 1944," in *Vnechnaia Politika Sovetskogo Soïouza*, vol. 2, (The Foreign Policy of the Soviet Union) (Moscow: Ogiz, 1946), 42.

2. Christian Fouchet, the French "delegate" in Warsaw, arrived in the Polish capital on December 23, 1944. He was to be replaced by March 16, 1945, by R. Garreau, coming from Moscow, who from June 29, 1945, was ambassador in Warsaw, after Paris had recognized (a few days before London and Washington!) the "Government of National Unity" in Poland.

to the Polish government that it make concessions on the
frontier issue, the latter might be induced to adopt a more
flexible position. From this starting point various transi-
tional solutions seemed possible. One of these, already
proposed on February 20, 1944, by Churchill in a message
to Stalin, consisted in fixing, pending the final settlement,
a "line of demarcation" between the Soviet and the Polish
administrations. This line was to follow a course close to
that claimed by the USSR, but which would leave to Poland
Lvov (and if possible Vilno), both towns with Polish majori-
ties. In any normal alliance (remember that it was a question of amputating an ally), such a proposal would have
seemed worthy of attention. This is what the prime minister
thought, while Roosevelt remained vague. But in his reply
to Churchill on March 3, Stalin, not content with rejecting
the "line of demarcation," reacted very strongly. The mere
fact of claiming the towns of Lvov and Vilno, he wrote, was
an "insult" to the Soviet government. No contact with the
Polish government could be considered so long as it had
not rid itself of the ministers rejected by the USSR.[3] When,
on March 7, Churchill replied that "force can achieve a
great deal, but force based on the good will of the world
can achieve even more." Stalin replied, on March 23, that
he could not yield before the threats of his ally. The
"threats," if one understands correctly, consisted in this:
that according to the language used by Churchill, the Soviet position rested on "force" alone, and not on "law."
According to Stalin, the law was the annexation by the
USSR of the western Ukraine and of western Byelorussia
on November 1 and 2, 1939, in response to the wishes of
assemblies "elected" in October in the two territories
which the Red Army had invaded six weeks earlier. What-

3. Cf. Llewellyn Woodward, *British Policy in the Second World War*, vol. 3
(London: HMS Office, 1971–1976), 178.

ever the nature of these "elections," they were worthless in international law. In this domain, the only text was that of the Ribbentrop-Molotov agreement of September 28, 1939, with which it would be difficult to confront an ally.

However, all did not seem lost. In Poland, the very first contacts between the Red Army and the Resistance were less bad than expected, particularly in Volhynia. In London, a dialogue was started between Victor Lebediev, USSR representative to the governments-in-exile, and key figures close to the Polish government. These contacts, spaced between March and July 1944, were concerned with conditions for a renewal of diplomatic relations which had been broken off by the USSR at the time of the discovery of the common graves of Katyn. If, to start with, an understanding did not seem out of the question, as time went by Soviet demands reappeared and increased: not only the "Curzon line," but also a Polish government with communist participation and a declaration whitewashing the USSR on Katyn. "Under those conditions," Mikolajczyk said to Lebediev, on June 23, "we have nothing more to say to each other."[4] And yet Sikorski's successors had understood that a compromise would have to be reached. But within certain limits.

When Mikolajczyk, backed if not pushed by Churchill and Roosevelt, went to see Stalin in early August 1944, he was pleasantly received but at the same time placed before two walls: the frontier claimed by Stalin and a "Polish Committee of National Liberation," which had surfaced in July at Lublin, the first large town to be occupied by the Red Army. Stalin referred Mikolajczyk back to this committee, which proposed a government in which the committee was to have fourteen ministers, and Mikolajczyk four! How could such obstacles be overcome? At this very moment,

4. Ibid., 3:193.

Warsaw, which had risen up on August 1 as the Soviet forces were approaching, was left to its fate. What had been a dispute became a tragedy.

The Warsaw Uprising

Born of the approach of the Soviet troops, the German threat to deport the male population capable of bearing arms, and of the irrepressible desire of the population to participate in the liberation of the capital, the uprising was, it seems, inevitable. Certainly audacious, doubtless foolhardy, the insurrection was a national tragedy whose effect is still felt today. It lasted two months, from August 1 to October 3, 1944, without receiving any support from the Soviet side save after September 15 (by which time the game was up for the Poles), a few parachute drops, and one or two attempts to cross the Vistula.

By early August, Stalin had condemned the insurrection as an adventure without any chance of success. Moreover, the possibility of landing behind the Soviet lines was denied to English or American planes charged with parachuting arms and ammunition to the insurgents. The negative attitude of the Soviet authorities greatly diminishes the validity of the criticism by those who thought that the insurgents, before launching their attack, should have established contact with the Red Army.[5] What would such contacts have produced? Was there any chance of the insurgents receiving effective support from the Soviet forces? Were these going to help them gain control of the capital while a Committee of Liberation, sponsored by Moscow and rival of the regular government-in-exile, ex-

5. Cf. J. M. Ciechanowski, *The Warsaw Rising of 1944* (Cambridge: Cambridge University Press, 1974), 259–260; and, closer to reality, the excellent analysis of Henry Rollet, in his book, *La Pologne au XXe siecle* (Paris: Pedone, 1984), 402–414.

isted in Lublin? The idea of the insurrection grew out of the Burza plan (Tempest), conceived by the leaders of the Resistance and endorsed by the Polish government in London. This plan sought to take advantage of the brief interval between the retreat of the Germans and the arrival of the Soviets to install the Resistance in key positions enabling them to welcome the "liberators." A plan of this kind involved considerable risks. But what else was there to do? What were the possibilities of agreement? Had the talks in the spring of 1944 revealed a basis for agreement, things would have been different. The prospect of an understanding, even though vague, would have made a certain degree of cooperation possible (as would be the case in France in August 1944, in spite of the strong differences between Roosevelt and de Gaulle). In the case of Poland, each time that there appeared a chance for an agreement, Stalin was careful not to seize it: he stuck to his demands, the frontier and a truly "independent" government, that is to say, "dependent" on friendship with the Soviet Union.[6] There was no margin and no opening. Had they existed, the offer of a "line of demarcation" in February and the insurrection in August could have seemed to Moscow to offer two opportunities worth seizing. Effective support of the insurrection would, in the long run have had considerable impact. The possibility of an authentic reconciliation might have loomed on the horizon. But Stalin held fast to his "realistic" line. There is nothing less realistic than absolute realism!

Among Stalin's motives, the first was doubtless the necessity of keeping the lid clamped down tight on the exactions and ravages committed between 1939 and 1941 in the Polish territories annexed by the USSR. One can also

6. Cf. Chapt. 2, 26, n. 14.

mention the fear of Ukrainian irredentism on the borders of the USSR, such as was to occur after 1945;[7] finally, one must take into account the nature of the Soviet regime: no reciprocity. "All animals are equal. Some animals are more equal than others."

This maxim of George Orwell does not apply only to Poland. In Yugoslavia, where circumstances were different, the USSR pursued the same policy.

Yugoslavia

Whereas Poland suffered in 1939 from German-Soviet collusion, Yugoslavia only suffered from Germany and Italy. The royal government took shelter in London (subsequently in Cairo), the Resistance split into two branches, which fought each other; one was national, with Draza Mihailovitch as war minister and the other was communist, under the control of Joseph Broz, called Tito, which Churchill had supplied and backed in 1942.

On November 1, 1944, an agreement was signed between Tito, president of the Yugoslav Committee of Liberation, and the head of the royal government-in-exile, Šubašić. This agreement provided for the setting up of a Regency Council (i.e., the elimination of the king, Peter II) and a government consisting of twenty-eight ministers, in which Tito's partisans were to have a substantial majority. This government "shall guarantee the implementation" of all democratic freedoms, and confirm the federal structure of the new Yugoslavia as created by the national Committee

---

7. N. S. Khrushchev, *Khrushchev Remembers*, ed. and tr. Strobe Talbot (Boston: Little, Brown & Co., 1970), 140. In French, *Souvenirs* (Paris: R. Laffont, 1971). Khrushchev speaks of the Ukrainian nationalist leader Bandera and of the armed Resistance, which continued in the Soviet Ukraine, several years after the end of the war.

of Liberation. In fact, the agreement gave Tito a free hand. This is why the king dissociated himself from it.

In the fall of 1944, difficulties multiplied between the Allies. These difficulties included blockage in Poland; entry of Soviet forces in Romania, Hungary, Bulgaria, and Yugoslavia; and blockage at the Dumbarton Oaks Conference, where the British, Americans, and Soviets laid down the broad lines of the future charter of the United Nations: The USSR claimed an unrestricted right of veto in the Security Council and the General Assembly in addition to the voice of the Soviet Union, those of the federated republics, which had recently become, according to the terms of a recent amendment to the Constitution of 1936, "autonomous" members of the union. Hence Churchill's trip to Moscow in the fall of 1944.

Churchill in Moscow
(October 9–18, 1944)

With Roosevelt at home in order to campaign for his fourth presidential mandate and Stalin refusing to leave his national soil, Churchill suggested that he go to Moscow to discuss current business. Stock was taken of the military situation and, as is usual in such meetings, views were exchanged on Germany—its future status and the possibility of its dismemberment—without, for all that, reaching firm conclusions. The actual negotiations concerned eastern Europe, Poland in the north, the Balkans in the south, and the Danubian basin as far as Hungary.

It is difficult to grasp what Churchill expected from this trip. While on a personal basis, relations between the British and the Soviets were quasi-cordial; in the political domain, the results were meager, if not bad. The agreement on the Balkans was meager, unsubstantial, and without much effect, placing Greece under British influence, Romania and Bulgaria under that of the Soviet Union, and establishing a proportionate influence in the adjacent countries, Yugoslavia and Hungary, all for a duration of three months, and based on a piece of paper on which Churchill had scribbled a few figures approved by Stalin with a pencil stroke. Behind this suggestion, which had already been made to Stalin four months earlier, but disapproved at the time by Roosevelt, lies the mutiny of the Greek fleet at Alexandria in March–April 1944. Churchill realized that the Soviet regime had a long reach, and that it could act far beyond the territories occupied by its forces. He therefore tried to prevent things from getting any worse. In fact, in December 1944 he put down the revolt of the EAM (National Liberation Front), which was an attempt to seize power by the communist-inspired Resistance. Stalin did not react, but later on, the civil war in Greece flared up again, and ended only in the fall of 1949, following the break between Stalin and Tito. Thus the agreement was of very relative scope. Even more ineffectual were the agreements involving Bulgaria, Yugoslavia, and Hungary, which were never carried out and never could be: what was meant by an influence of 25 or 30 percent? How could this be estimated?

The agreement on the Balkans may have saved Greece. As for the rest, it had no effect. As regards Poland, on the other hand, Churchill, who was anxious to conclude, not only confirmed his acceptance of the frontier which Stalin called the Curzon line, but applied intense and sometimes brutal pressure on Mikolajczyk whom he summoned to Moscow, where there were already members of the Polish Committee of National Liberation (PCLN), Bierut, Osobka-Morawski, etc. They, with Stalin's backing, agreed to enlarge their committee by the addition of noncommunist leaders, but on condition of keeping, as in the Yugoslav model, almost all the seats. Faced with the Soviet demands, which Churchill considered reasonable, Mikolajczyk ended by accepting both the Curzon line and his participation in a preponderantly communist provisional government, that is to say, the two major demands of the USSR ever since the Polish-Soviet agreements were negotiated by Sikorski in London in July 1941. No doubt Churchill thought that it was just a stage, that peace would follow, and that Poland would be able to revive gradually. But he had gone a long way down the road of concessions. Mikolajczyk was repudiated by his ministers on his return to London and resigned. The road now lay open before the Bierut government. More accurately, the road was open four months after Yalta when in June 1945, Hopkins, Roosevelt's former confidant now under instructions from Truman, delivered the concessions demanded by Stalin in order to make sure of his hold on Poland.

It is easy to criticize Britain's policy forty years later. Anthony Eden summed it up in one sentence: "Poland . . . was the ally for whose sake we had gone to war with Germany, yet whose territory was most remote from us."[8] As we shall see later, the Polish problem lay at the heart of the discussions at Yalta, and after Yalta. It is true that Poland could have been better supported with stronger arguments based on more concrete countermeasures. For this the Western leaders would have had to have a more accurate perception both of the Soviet regime and of Stalin as a person. What appears obvious today was apparent to hardly anyone in 1944–1945, that is to say at a time when everything was still in abeyance. This can be seen if we recall the conditions under which the Franco-Soviet pact of mutual assistance was concluded in Moscow in December 1944.

8. A. Eden, *The Reckoning* (London: Cassell, 1965), 506.

The Franco-Soviet Pact
(December 10, 1944)

From 1940 to 1945, Free France, Fighting France, and then the French Committee for National Liberation had serious difficulties with Great Britain concerning the overseas territories, as well as in many other fields; they also had difficulties with the United States, present at Vichy until the end of 1942 and entertaining strong reservations before and after that date toward General de Gaulle. This generated in the latter a quasi-irresistible urge to look to the East for support. In Moscow, the Delegation of Free France multiplied its overtures; criticized the major Western Allies, suspected of passivity if not bad faith; and attributed to them dark designs concerning the European Resistance movements. In London, General de Gaulle, while looking at the situation in a more detached way, was rarely positive in his judgments on those he called the "Anglo-Saxons." We find an example of this in his remarks in May 1944 to Bogomolov, the ambassador of the USSR, whom de Gaulle had invited to lunch at Tipaza, 70 kilometers from Algiers.[9] "The ultimate aim of British policy," he said, "is revealed in the current thinking of the Anglo-Americans: to establish their control over France and her government as metropolitan France is being liberated."

9. "Meeting between de Gaulle and Bogomolov," in *Sovetsko-Frantsuzskie Otnocheniia (1941–1945)*, vol. 2 (Moscow, 1983), Doc. 25, 55–59. A. Harriman and E. Abel in *Special Envoy to Churchill and Stalin* (New York: Random House, 1975), 231–232, comment on a conversation between Harriman and General de Gaulle at Algiers on October 15, 1943:

He spoke of France and Russia as the only two powerful countries in Europe, after the collapse of Germany. The British, after all, would retire to their islands and the Americans would go home across the Atlantic. Thus the future of Europe, as he saw it, would be determined by France and Russia working together. "We cannot depend upon the help of Great Britain and the United States, and therefore French policy should be tied to Soviet policy."

We have no confidence in England, not even when
she speaks to us of an alliance with France. . . .
France needs an alliance with Russia and a series of
European states contiguous to Germany, Holland,
Belgium, Austria, Czechoslovakia, Poland. The
essential goal of this alliance is to settle the German
problem. Neither England nor the United States
wants Germany to be weakened too much. England
is prepared to flatter Germany. If Russia wants to
settle the German problem once and for all, she can
do it only by relying on the support of France and
the other democratic countries of the European
continent.

"On his departure for London," concluded the ambassador, "de Gaulle wants to be able to count on our support
in case of a serious disagreement with Churchill and the
Americans. . . . But de Gaulle also harbors a real grudge
against the British who tend to talk down to him."

As Bogomolov said, it is understandable that General
de Gaulle, snubbed by the West, should have had a tendency to turn toward the East. But this shift has a deeper
origin. The postwar plans developed in Algiers grew out of
the Franco-Soviet alliance of 1893: Germany was to be held
fast in a Franco-Soviet vise; a Germanic confederation, as
weak as possible, would replace the Reich; the left bank of
the Rhine would be under French control, the Ruhr basin
under international control. These views could not dis-
please Moscow. However, the Soviet leaders were more
interested in the powerful, than in the convalescent, allies.

It was, therefore, the head of the French government
who took the initiative on November 8. Following an inter-
view with Bogomolov, "de Gaulle said that he would like
to go to the Soviet Union with a few of his ministers, if this
were convenient to the Soviet government, in order to

examine the relations between the two countries.[10] On November 14, the invitation arrived.[11] The general and the delegation accompanying him spent a week in Moscow from December 2 to 10, 1944.

A pact was mentioned at the opening session. According to the French delegation's version, it was Stalin who first brought up the matter. Indeed, Stalin said during the first session, in very general terms, that a good alliance was worth more than the best strategic frontiers, in this case the Rhine, which de Gaulle had mentioned, receiving only an evasive reply from Stalin. But even before the arrival of the French, Stalin questioned Churchill and Roosevelt about the proposed alliance which, according to his information, the French intended to air. The French delegation, moreover, had brought with it a draft treaty, which it transmitted to the Soviets on December 3 and which was very close to the Soviet counterproposal handed to the French delegation a few days later. There is no doubt that there had been preliminary contacts.[12]

As soon as the idea of an alliance had been injected into the discussion, there appeared another underlying problem, that of Poland. It was raised by Molotov in his first

10. In *Sovetsko-Frantsuzskie*, vol. 2, Doc. 69, 139.

11. "Taking into account the wish, expressed by General de Gaulle in a conversation with Ambassador Bogomolov on November 8, 1944, and according to whose terms the General wishes to visit the USSR in order to establish a personal contact with the leaders of the Soviet government, the Soviet government receives this proposal favorably and invites General de Gaulle to come to the USSR" (letter from Bogomolov to General de Gaulle, November 14, 1944, Archives of the Ministry of Foreign Affairs, Paris).

12. Telegram No. 86 addressed to Moscow by the minister of foreign affairs, November 24, 1944: "Finally, I am bringing with me background papers enabling me to raise, and to push ahead with as far as the Soviet government might wish, the study of contractual relations between France and the USSR" (Archives of the Ministry of Foreign Affairs, Paris).

conversation with Bidault, on December 5. Why should France not appoint a delegate to the Polish Committee of National Liberation (PCNL) installed in Warsaw? General de Gaulle replied on December 7 that he did not consider it desirable to break with the Polish government-in-exile so long as the situation in Poland was not really clear. In the meantime, a member of the Soviet delegation pointed out to one of his French colleagues that France could establish a "direct contact" in Warsaw with the PCNL without thereby modifying its relations with the Polish government in London. "The Soviet government has for some time had de facto relations with the Italian government," the French government could act in a similar manner in regard to the PCNL.[13]

Thus the trail had not been merely cleared, but blazed. However, with the French turning a deaf ear, a new obstacle arose: on December 7, Stalin received a favorable reply from Churchill concerning an alliance between France and the USSR, but also suggesting the idea of an Anglo-Franco-Soviet pact. On December 7, Molotov stressed the advantages of a tripartite pact, which obviously could not be concluded in forty-eight hours. With the French lining up arguments against a tripartite pact, negotiations on the Polish question were pursued behind the scenes. When, on December 8, General de Gaulle accepted the idea of de facto relations with the PCNL, the tripartite project went up in smoke. There remained the final haggling: "official" or "unofficial" representatives? During the night of December 9–10, after long discussions, an agreement was reached: the delegates were to be "unofficial." There was indeed some resistance from the French side, but it concerned form rather than substance. The first representative of a democratic government accredited to the Polish au-

13. "Conversation between Mr. Dejean and Mr. G. Gergueier, on December 5, 1945," in *Sovetsko-Frantsuzskie,* vol. 2, 516.

thority installed in Warsaw by the USSR—an unofficial representative, but a representative nonetheless—was thus to be a Frenchman. When Churchill complained at Yalta of not being able to send an observer to Poland to keep him informed, Stalin retorted, "De Gaulle has a representative there, why not do the same?"[14] In the same way, but with more success, Stalin pressured Beneš to recognize the provisional Polish government early in 1945.

This analysis does not contradict the one we find in the *Mémoires de guerre:* "Stalin was going to try to sell us the pact in exchange for our public endorsement of his Polish operation."[15] This is by and large what happened, the endorsement being as discreet as possible. But the analysis diverges from the *Mémoires* to the extent that, from a distance and according to documents published in Moscow, it seems that the Soviets were prepared to be satisfied with an exchange of "unofficial" representatives between Paris and Warsaw. The battle was less serious than had seemed at the time.

It remains to ask ourselves what the compensation was worth. Was the Franco-Soviet alliance indispensable at that time? What advantages could one expect from it? Here we must distinguish between domestic and foreign policy.

Internally, given the state of confusion in France at the time of the liberation, drawing closer to Moscow could have a beneficial effect: in the fall of 1944 there existed, notably in the Communist party, a tendency to oppose the National Resistance Council to the provisional government.[16] This tendency did not develop further. Maurice

14. SANO, vol. 2, 271.

15. C. de Gaulle, *Mémoires de guerre,* vol. 3 (Paris: Plon, 1959), 167.

16. Telegram from René Massigli, ambassador in London, sent to Paris, October 6, 1944:

I have just learned from a very reliable source that on his way through Algiers, the ambassador [M. Bogomolov] had a talk with a member of the British embassy who had remained there. The official gave an account of the conversa-

Thorez, back from his Muscovite exile on November 30, 1944, chose in his first speech the line of republican legality, from which the Communist party incidentally derived an advantage, a line which the alliance of December 10 could only strengthen.[17] Let us stress that there had, of course, been no dealings with Stalin on this subject. The latter was in any case too busy implanting his regime in the form of popular democracy in eastern Europe where he pulled all the strings.

But what was the pact worth from the viewpoint of foreign policy? As we know, the alliance of 1944 was denounced by the USSR in 1955, when the Federal Republic of Germany joined the Atlantic alliance. No one became in the least excited. It is true that in 1944 one could not foresee the great turnarounds of the postwar period. But one might have wondered as early as 1944 about the nature of the commitments made in Moscow. According to the text of Articles 3 and 4 of the pact, assistance was mandatory, not merely as in the Anglo-Soviet treaty of May 26, 1942, in case of German aggression against one of the signatories, but also if one of the parties became involved in hostilities with Germany for having taken "all necessary measures to eliminate any new threat originating in Germany." In other words, in the event of preventive war, an extremely onerous obligation which risked subordinating the less powerful of the two signatories to the will of the other. Even more serious was the fact that a similar clause existed in the Soviet-Czech pact of December 12, 1943, a clause which was also to appear in the treaties signed by the

---

tion in a report which was summarized for me as follows: "The Soviet government is playing the Resistance card—I was told even the Council of the Resistance—against the provisional government" (Archives of the Ministry of Foreign Affairs, Paris).

17. Cf. S. Courtois, *Le PCF dans la guerre* (Paris: Ramsay, 1980), 466–467.

USSR with the Yugoslav government of Marshal Tito on April 11 and with the provisional Polish government on April 21, 1945. Between 1943 and 1945, the USSR progressively built up a security system on the European continent, a system based not on resistance to aggression but on preventing aggression. Suppose that, as Roosevelt said at Yalta, the United States had withdrawn from Europe two years after the victory, how could such a system have failed to be dominated by the USSR?

One can reply to these remarks that, at the time, only the German danger was feared in France. However it seems that at the Quai d'Orsay, Jean Chauvel, the Secretary General, warned the provisional government against any strictly continental security system. He briefly mentioned his reservations to the writer of these lines as the delegation was departing at Orly on November 24. He repeated them in a telegram to Moscow on December 1, 1944, referring to an article in *l'Humanité,* according to which "the Franco-Soviet alliance should not necessarily be considered as falling within the framework of the Anglo-Soviet alliance." "It is hardly necessary," Chauvel wrote, "to emphasize the continental character of this position."[18] A tactful but clear warning!

So what should have been done? Without claiming to reconstruct the past, one may feel that a trip unencumbered by the negotiation of an alliance might, following on a less taut exchange of views, have ended with a communiqué announcing that negotiations aimed at a postwar security system would open in the near future. Internally, the effect would have been the same. Externally, there would have been time to reflect, to discuss and to negotiate, and the result might have been a text better suited to reality. Simultaneously, one would have avoided the dif-

18. Telegram No. 116 sent to Moscow, December 1, 1944 (Archives of the Ministry of Foreign Affairs, Paris).

ficulty in regard to Poland that was raised in Moscow. For that, a revelation of the future would have been required which, while focusing on Germany, was a little less molded by the past, distant or recent: Bismarck, Wilhelm II, or Hitler. France's policy after the end of the fighting could more easily have looked toward the future.

On the Eve of Yalta
(January 1945)

Seen from Moscow, Europe was a field of ruins. On this devastated continent, if one is to believe the Soviet history manuals, a powerful "revolutionary" movement was growing which the Western Allies wanted to stifle and which the Soviet Union could only encourage.[19] To the north, since the armistice with Finland, there was no major obstacle in the way of the USSR. At the most, by landing on Bornholm in April 1945, the Soviet Union attempted to establish control over the Danish straits at the entrance of the Baltic. To the south, domination over the Balkans appeared more or less ensured, and Stalin raised the matter of the Black Sea straits with Churchill in August 1944. To the west, in France, Belgium, and Italy, active Communist parties were able to exert pressure on the policy of newly installed governments. Finally, in the center, Germany was on the verge of collapse. Before the USSR stretched the key axis of its security: Moscow, Warsaw, Berlin, and beyond.

To Harriman, who expressed his pleasure at seeing

19. Cf., for example, A. A. Gromyko and B. Ponomarev, eds., *History of the Foreign Policy of the USSR,* vol. 1, *1917–1945* (in Russian) (Moscow: Nauka Editions, 1976), 471:

> The revolutionary processes in eastern Europe were strongly aimed at the capitalistic system and powerful imperialistic interests. This is why the American and British governments were striving, with all their means, to oppose the development of the revolution. This was especially true because the revolutionary movement could have likewise developed in countries that had been liberated by the Western Powers.

Stalin at Potsdam, Stalin replied: "Tsar Alexander got as far as Paris."[20] One should not exaggerate the significance of this reply, which may merely have been a sally, but however one interprets it, it implies a policy which embraces the entire continent. As early as 1945, the USSR, while laying the basis for a bloc of "popular democracy," manifested its hostility to the idea of a "Western bloc." In Moscow, Stalin warned de Gaulle on this subject. He did not have in mind a partition but a gradual movement by stages, prudent certainly, but continuous.

The view from London: Europe was threatened by the weight of the victorious USSR whose armies, while rolling back the enemy, helped to set up unpopular regimes in the liberated countries as well as in the conquered ones. More than anyone, Churchill was worried by this upheaval. Having been unable in 1944 to gain acceptance for his plan of a thrust toward Vienna through the Ljubljana gap, he had to confine himself to saving Greece *in extremis.* But what was to be done in the center? Germany no longer existed and Stalin was certainly alone in imagining that in the final act, the British and the Americans were going to come to terms with the enemy in order to turn against the USSR. Thus it was France which Churchill saw as the breakwater of resistance to a resurgence of aggressiveness in Germany and, above all, to Soviet expansion on the Continent, which in his mind presupposed the support and the presence of the United States.[21]

The view from Paris: Europe must prepare itself to become one day "the arbiter between the two camps, Soviet and Anglo-Saxon." France, while concluding the "nec-

20. A. Szombati, "Harriman, interlocuteur de Staline," *Le Monde-Dimanche,* December 14, 1980; and A. Harriman, *America and Russia in a Changing World* (New York: Doubleday & Co., 1971), 44.

21. Letter to Roosevelt, November 19, 1944, in Francis Loewenheim and Harold D. Langley, *Roosevelt and Churchill, Their Secret Wartime Correspondence* (New York: Dutton, 1975), 602–603.

essary alliances," must succeed in grouping together "the states which border on the Rhine, the Alps, the Pyrenees" in order to prevent another Reich from being able once again to threaten her.[22] The implementation of these very broad views led France to try to weaken what remained of Germany as much as possible and to pursue in the immediate postwar period a policy equidistant from the "two camps" but, for that very reason, very far removed from reality.

"For Germany," Raymond Aron wrote, as early as 1946, "the year 1945 was what 1815 had been for France." In other words, the danger was no longer German, it lay further to the east.

In Washington, Roosevelt remained true to his world design: to win the confidence of the USSR by granting it a sufficiently large area of expansion and creating a security system which, thanks to a good understanding between Americans and Soviets, would guarantee peace for many years. No more than Churchill did Roosevelt grasp the implications of the problem created by Stalin's policy in Poland. He was not very sensitive to the specific particulars of equilibrium on a world scale; he did not clearly comprehend the nature of the Soviet regime, even less the extreme peculiarity of its leader.

On the eve of Yalta, Anthony Eden noted in his diary on January 4, 1945: "I am much worried that the whole business will be chaotic and nothing worth while settled, Stalin being the only one of the three who has a clear view of what he wants and is a tough negotiator. P.M. is all emotion on these matters, F.D.R. vague and jealous of others."[23]

22. C. de Gaulle, *Mémoires,* vol. 3, 180–181.

23. A. Eden, *The Reckoning,* 583.

5

The Crimea Conference
(February 4–11, 1945)

To NEGOTIATE IS TO HAGGLE. "Let us make mutual concessions."[1] Yalta is no exception to this rule. But in its application, one should note a difference between the East and the West which often passes unnoticed. Whatever their ambitions, their mental reservations, the British and especially the Americans instinctively thought of peace as the return to normal life: Whether resisting or yielding in the course of discussion, this was in order to attempt to reach some form of agreement assumed to be advantageous to everyone. With their interlocutor it was a different matter: he certainly desired an end to the conflict but for him, this end did not (and doubtless could not) signify a return to peace, still less to good understanding. It was not possible for rivalries not to reemerge, thus it was a matter of accumulating gains and advantages. One side groped around for compromises which, after the victory, should at least permit at a minimum a certain equilibrium. The other was preparing for inevitable confrontations.

---

1. English equivalent of an old French saying: *"Passe-moi la casse, je te passerai le séné."*

At that game, Stalin greatly risked compromising the future in exchange for certain immediate and tangible gains. The risk was all the greater in that never, neither at Tehran nor since, was he ever given a serious warning. Churchill was tempted to do so one evening in Moscow, on October 11, 1944, but after thinking it over he held onto the letter which had been drafted to Stalin.[2] The one he wrote on April 29, 1945, which he sent off, leaves nothing unsaid about his concerns. "There is not much comfort," he writes, "in looking into a future where you and the countries you dominate, plus the Communist parties in many other states, are all drawn up on one side, and those who rally to the English-speaking nations and their associates or dominions are on the other. It is quite obvious that their quarrel would tear the world to pieces and that all of us leading men on either side who had anything to do with that would be shamed before history."[3] But, isolated, could Churchill make himself heard? Roosevelt did little in his correspondence to warn Stalin against a lasting disagreement after the war.

Misunderstandings were all the more to be feared because the conference was not preceded by any tripartite preparation. The stakes at issue would have been more visible if the ministers of foreign affairs had met together before the meeting of the top leaders, not only to work out an agenda but also to sketch out their respective positions in a document that would reveal areas of disagreement so that, at the moment of decision, each one would know whether he stood on firm ground or on the brink of the precipice.

Stalin, from what we know of him, was hardly inclined to show his hand prematurely. Roosevelt, mistrust-

2. W. Churchill, *The Second World War*, vol. 6 (Boston: Houghton Mifflin, 1950), 231–233.

3. Ibid., 494–497. See Appendix B, in this volume, for the integral text of Churchill's letter and Stalin's reply.

ful of the State Department, had set as his principal goal
the creation of a climate of confidence between himself
and Stalin. An impossible task! Churchill found himself
between two mighty partners, both conscious that their
agreement left the third little latitude. To which must
be added a few concrete facts: Roosevelt, who presided,
tended to assume the role of arbiter between Stalin and
Churchill; the quarters of the three delegations were more
than 10 kilometers away from each other, which rendered
impossible the informal contacts which are often valuable
in these kinds of meetings; moreover, Roosevelt intended
to leave the Black Sea on February 11 at the latest. Time
was limited.

And France, one will ask? Why was she not at Yalta?
The facts are known. On January 15, 1945, the provisional
government delivered a lengthy note to her three allies,
asking that she be invited to the meeting which was being
prepared. The British had envisaged partial participation
by France—for example, at the end of the conference.
Roosevelt hesitated. Stalin said nothing.

The French *démarche* was unusual: to ask in writing to
be invited is to concede that there is little chance that one
will be. It is true that in the interallied organizations, especially those relating to Germany, France was reassuming in
late 1944 the responsibilities which she was seeking. But
what could France's representative have achieved at Yalta?
In what way could he have influenced decisions? What policy would he have advocated in regard to Germany? Bound
by an alliance to the Soviet Union for the postwar period,
what else could he have observed than that he did not count
for much in the eyes of his allies? By what means could he
have succeeded in making his point of view prevail? As we
know, it was at the Yalta Conference that, thanks to the
efforts of Churchill and Eden, France was invited to occupy
a zone in Germany, to sit on the Control Council in Berlin,
to become a permanent member of the Security Council of
the United Nations, and in short, to recover her place in the

international arena. These results were more important
than those which a jump seat at the conference would have
brought her.

The Stakes

The negotiations concerned first and foremost *Europe,*
in regard to which Stalin had specific, but unavowed intentions; the *Far East,* the object of territorial claims by the
Soviet Union; and finally, the *organization of future peace,*
Roosevelt's chief concern.

Europe

In the Balkans and central Europe, the surrender of
Romania and Bulgaria in the fall of 1944 and that of Hungary in January 1945 already ensured for the Soviet Union
a preponderant role which, thanks to Tito and the Yugoslav
partisans, extended to the confines of Italy. The British and
Americans were not satisfied with the functioning of the
armistice commissions on which their representatives were
mere onlookers. In Poland there was the East-West confrontation: two Polish governments; two Resistance networks; two rival armies, one in the west, the other in the
USSR; and the national territory in the hands of one of the
states represented at the conference. In Yugoslavia,
Churchill, who had backed Tito long before Stalin showed
any interest in him, tried to restore unity. In November
1944, the royal government-in-exile sent Prime Minister
Šubašić to negotiate an agreement with Tito with the aim
of creating a unified government, an agreement more favorable to Tito than to Šubašić now had to be implemented.[4] The tension was less dramatic than in Poland, but
was of the same kind.

4. See Chapt. 4, 49.

In Germany, there was to be no government for as long as the Three had not otherwise decided. Unconditional surrender, the idea Roosevelt had rashly launched at Casablanca in 1943, created a vacuum in the heart of Europe.

France, although liberated, had not yet found her place again. Churchill backed France, Roosevelt distrusted her, and Stalin despised her: in 1940 "she did not fight," and in 1945, like Poland, she had only a "provisional government" and at the most "a few divisions" that were combat ready.

In Europe, Stalin, who thought less in terms of influence than of hardware or networks, could in 1945 envisage a policy extending as far as the shores of the Atlantic, thanks to the Communist parties and their ramifications. Roosevelt had no European policy worthy of the name; his basic concern was to keep up good personal relations with Stalin, to obtain the support of the Soviet forces in the Far East, and to create the organization of the United Nations. Churchill saw ill omens accumulating: in order to contain the USSR, he tried to obtain support from a reviving France, tried not to permit the fragmentation of Germany, and tried to retain a measure of influence in the countries to the east. But could England alone offset the weight of the Soviet Union? France had barely emerged from the depths, Germany no longer existed, and central and eastern Europe were in the hands of the Soviet Union. Hitlerian nihilism had left nothing standing of the European prewar structure. In February 1945, it was difficult to conceive what tomorrow's Europe would be like and more difficult still to rebuild it.

United Nations

As we have seen above,[5] the creation of the United Nations, which was destined to take the place of the League

5. See Chapt. 4, 50.

of Nations (from which the USSR was expelled in 1939 for having attacked Finland), was the object of negotiations in the fall of 1944 at Dumbarton Oaks in Washington, D.C., first between the Three Powers, then between the United States, England, and China.[6] Two disagreements remained between the Soviet Union and its Western Allies. One of these concerned what was called the right of veto, that is to say, the necessity of a unanimous vote of the five permanent members of the Security Council for a decision to be taken; the other concerned the method of voting in the General Assembly.

In the Security Council, the USSR claimed an unlimited right of veto. The Americans and the British suggested a compromise: the right of veto would not apply when it was a matter of procedure (e.g., inscription of a question on the agenda); likewise, in a case when one of the five was itself party to a disagreement which was the object of a pacific mode of settlement.

In the General Assembly, the USSR asked for seventeen votes (that of the Union plus the "autonomous" republics), a request which seemed exhorbitant. There was no compromise in sight. Roosevelt and his favorite adviser, Hopkins, saw in these Soviet claims a major obstacle on the road to peace. How could such privileges be reconciled with the principle of equality between the states?

The Far East

Here the differences were smaller. The United States insisted on intervention by the USSR in the last phase of the war against Japan. Stalin had given assurances on this point as early as 1943, while letting it be understood that he would need important territorial advantages in Northeast Asia as compensation. Short of this, he asserted, "pub-

6. In order not to "provoke" Japan, the USSR preferred not to sit at the same table as China.

lic opinion" in the USSR would not understand this pro-
longation of the war. This problem was discussed outside
the conference itself, directly between Roosevelt and Stalin. The advantages promised to the USSR in Northern
China and Japan do not appear in the overall record of the
meeting.

As a result of this, the actual negotiation—the balance struck between demands and concessions—involved
only two areas: the *European continent,* of which the USSR
already occupied a large portion, and the *United Nations,*
which Roosevelt considered the foundation of the future
peace.

The Maneuvers

Every negotiation, whatever its nature, is a question of
timing. He who knows which move to make at the right
moment gains more than he who confines himself to maintaining his position. This rule was confirmed at the Yalta
Conference, in which one can identify three phases: the
setting up of the plan of action, the decisive confrontation,
and the outcome.

From Sunday, February 4, to Tuesday, February 6,
Churchill, Roosevelt, and Stalin exchanged views in accordance with the agenda: Germany, Poland, and the
United Nations. On Tuesday evening, they found themselves at a dead end on Poland and the United Nations,
both key questions.

On Wednesday, the 7th, Stalin seized the initiative.
From the very beginning of the session, he abandoned, or
in any case greatly reduced, his demands concerning the
veto in the Security Council and the plurality vote in the
U.N. General Assembly. As compensation, he won ap-
proval in principle of a text on Poland, cleverly drafted
while conforming to his position. The ground lost was
never recovered.

The following three days were taken up by hard-fought discussions about Poland, Germany (especially reparations), and incidentally, France and the place it should occupy after the war. The British, forming a square, tried to resist, but when American support was not forthcoming, they had, for the most part, to conform to the concessions granted by the latter. During the negotiations, Roosevelt and Stalin reached agreement on the Far East during two private conversations on February 8 and 10.[7]

The Negotiations

Germany

The German problem was on the agenda of the second session on Monday, the 5th (the first studied forecasts and the strategic plans in Europe and the Pacific). In fact, Germany as such was not discussed, because by virtue of unconditional surrender, Germany would no longer legally exist after the defeat and would be at the mercy of the victors. All would depend on the degree of agreement they would be able to reach between them. But the necessity for agreement would assert itself better if, after the defeat, there existed some kind of responsible German authority which would have to be reckoned with. Failing such an authority, each would be master in his own zone, and the risks of divergences, not to say confrontation, would be serious.

The discussion of Germany was limited to a few specific points without ever dealing with the whole picture. Stalin raised three questions: the dismemberment of Germany; the consequences of surrender (should a government be established in Germany?); and reparations. To

7. See below, 80.

which Roosevelt added the problem of the French zone of occupation.

It emerged from the discussion that, according to Stalin, the act of surrender should mention the possibility of dismemberment and that one should not permit a new German government to be created immediately following the cessation of hostilities. The Soviet plan for reparations, put forward by Maiski, provided for a total financial claim of $20 billion, of which $10 billion were for the USSR levied in the form of dismantled factories, delivery of goods over a period of ten years, and German labor transferred to, or retained in, the USSR.

Churchill was opposed, not to dismemberment, but the mention of it in the act of surrender. On the one hand, this should be given careful consideration; on the other, one risked needlessly prolonging German resistance. The best thing to do was to refer the task of studying the question to a working group. "[T]he fate of eighty million people . . . required more than eighty minutes to consider."[8] Roosevelt was not opposed to dismemberment. As for Stalin, he specified what he was after. He insisted on dismemberment being *mentioned* in the text of surrender. One would see later about carrying it out.

From this insistence, one could deduce his real objective: if the act of surrender provided explicitly for the dismemberment of Germany, the Western Allies would find it difficult to come to terms at the last minute with some German general. What Stalin wanted was to obtain a guarantee against his "allies." He revealed this when, in discussing the eventuality of a group of plotters overthrowing Hitler, he wondered whether one would have to discuss matters "with those people, as had been the case in Italy

---

8. *Foreign Relations of the USA, The Conferences at Malta and Yalta* (Washington, D.C.: Government Printing Office, 1955), 614.

with Badoglio."[9] The question of dismemberment was referred to the ministers of foreign affairs. Then the matter
dragged on. It was taken up again on the side in London
during the March session of the European Advisory Commission. Then, one day at the end of March, the Soviet
representative announced unexpectedly that his government had abandoned the idea of dismemberment. This is
what Stalin was to state on May 8, 1945; he had already
hinted at this as early as February 1942.[10]

Insofar as one can understand, this was a maneuver
with several ends in view: to prevent any collusion of the
Western powers with some German authority born of the
disaster; to take advantage, meanwhile, of this decision in
principle in order to amputate unilaterally eastern Germany; and perhaps even (this was Charles Bohlen's idea in
his memoirs[11]) to saddle the Western Allies at an appropriate moment with responsibility for dismemberment.

On the subject of reparations, Roosevelt and Stalin
reached agreement (not without reservations): yes, in principle, to the $10 billion in favor of the USSR, but as a "basis
for discussion," the agreement remaining conditional.
Churchill, having even stronger reservations, refused to
commit himself. The question of reparations was referred
to a tripartite commission, which was to meet in Moscow
in the spring without much result. This debate on reparations didn't bring the USSR everything it had demanded.
But since the principle had been accepted, it was able to
help itself from the territories it occupied.

As for France, the Three agreed to set aside a zone of
occupation for her (even though Roosevelt confided to
Stalin that this was purely out of "the goodness of his

9. Ibid., p. 615.

10. See Chapt. 1, 11–12.

11. C. E. Bohlen, *Witness to History* (New York: Norton & Co., 1973), 183.

heart"[12]). But up to the last day, Roosevelt and Stalin refused to allow a French representative to sit on the Allied
Control Council in Berlin. Roosevelt did not like General
de Gaulle. Stalin, who manifested little regard for France
in his statements, doubtless tried to keep in reserve the
possibility of a concession *in extremis*. Perhaps he also had
an idea in the back of his mind concerning this case. During
the entire conference he had established a close parallel
between France and Poland. If France were called on to
administer a zone in Germany without being seated on the
Allied Control Council, would this not constitute a precedent for what he was to do one month later, in March, when
he installed, without having consulted anyone, a Polish
administration in the German territories to the east of the
Oder-Neisse line? However this may be, when, on the last
day, Roosevelt, who had been admonished by his advisers,
consented to let France sit on the Control Council, Stalin
replied with a single word, "Sdaious!" (I give up!). Churchill and Eden had chalked up a point.

The discussion on Germany was only preliminary.
There was agreement on negative principles, surrender,
denazification, and demilitarization, not on a policy. Seen
with the perspective of the years which had elapsed since
1945, this discussion revealed the flaw which was to result
in the division of Germany: in the absence of common
views on the future, how could unity be preserved? However, nothing had yet been decided. At Yalta, Stalin was
confirmed in his distrust of Churchill, the latter in his pessi-

12. One will note that at Yalta it was Stalin who raised the question of
dismemberment. Churchill was reticent, Roosevelt rather favorably disposed. In
their *History of the Foreign Policy of the USSR* (Moscow: Nauka Editions, 1976),
Anatole Gromyko and Boris Ponomarev write, "During the Crimea Conference,
the English and American leaders again spoke in favor of dismemberment of
Germany" (481). And further on, "Thanks to the USSR, the question of the
dismemberment of Germany was struck from the agenda for the interallied discussions" (482).

mism for the future. Roosevelt stood between the two. This new configuration of the alliance, with Churchill on one side, Stalin on the other, and Roosevelt in the middle became clearer when it came to the question of Poland.

Poland

The two major questions in the eyes of the participants, the United Nations and Poland, were on the agenda for Tuesday, February 6. Stalin, who had long since received a compromise formula on the issue of the vote at the United Nations, declared himself unable to conclude on this point and called for further explanations. And thus we come to the Polish question: how to find a remedy for the existence of two rival governments? Which (western) boundaries should be given to the new Poland?[13]

The president of the United States, drawing on a suggestion by Stanislaw Mikolajczyk, proposed that a *Presidential Council* be set up, a kind of regency council whose task would be to *"form* a government consisting of representatives of the five principal political parties," thus including the communists. Churchill went along, the essential factor in his view being that Poland remain "independent," "captain of her soul." Stalin emphasized that there already existed a government in Poland and that this government was good, popular, and effective, whereas the one in London was bad, reactionary, and anti-Soviet. He added that over the centuries Poland had been the "corridor of invasions from the west." It was thus a matter of security for the USSR. Churchill replied that his reports were very different from those of the marshal and that it was out of the question for him to recognize the "Lublin government." The discussion ended without having reached a conclusion.

---

13. On this point, the Three confirmed, in the final communiqué, their agreement on the Curzon line as the eastern frontier of Poland, but left in abeyance the line of the western frontier suggested by the USSR and that, in Churchill's view, cut too deeply into the territory of Germany.

It is strange that there should have been no one to recall that in August 1914, as in June 1941, the Germans and Russians were confronting each other on Poland's territory, which had been divided between them the first time from 1795 to 1919 and again in September 1939. In both cases, Poland was innocent, since it had ceased to exist as a state.

In the evening of February 6 Roosevelt prepared, with Bohlen's help, a draft letter to Stalin, which he got the English to approve.[14] Asserting his intention to "avoid any breach between the United States and the Soviet Union," Roosevelt suggested that a certain number of Poles, representing all tendencies, be brought to Yalta who would reach an accord on the formation of a "new provisional government" which could be recognized by the Three Powers. The president was thus maintaining a firm position. But he allowed his desire to reach a compromise to be too evident. At the session on the following day, Wednesday the 7th, Stalin said that he had received Roosevelt's letter, that he had tried without success to reach "by telephone" some of the key Polish figures listed by the president, but that, nevertheless, Molotov had prepared a few suggestions on Poland whose text was not yet typed. Stalin therefore suggested starting with a debate on the question of the United Nations. Molotov immediately took the floor; he stated that the compromise on the right of veto proposed the previous day by the American delegation[15] was, after reflection, entirely acceptable. This was the first turnabout! He added that so far as the federated republics were concerned, the USSR was prepared to be content with the admission to the General Assembly of three, or even only two. What had seemed, the previous day, to be an insuperable obstacle disappeared almost entirely. For Roosevelt,

14. *The Conferences at Malta and Yalta,* 727.

15. See above, 68.

although granting three votes to the USSR (those of the USSR and two republics) was unfortunate;[16] the road lay clear toward the United Nations, through which he saw the means of putting an end to U.S. isolationism and hence the guarantee of the future peace. The resulting effect of decompression was considerable.

After a brief pause, Molotov put forward the Soviet proposal on Poland. This document defined, in six points, the eastern and western frontiers of the future Poland and proposed that the provisional Polish government, i.e., the Lublin government, which had established itself in Warsaw on January 17, should be "enlarged" by adding to it a few "democratic leaders" from among the "ranks of Polish émigrés." Roosevelt and Churchill found, each in his own way, that this represented important progress. And yet, if one leaves aside the buildup, the Soviet proposal contributed little that was new: the provisional government established by the USSR was to be increased by "a few" members, would be recognized by the Three, and "would call on the population to vote as soon as possible." This amounted to confirming, not modifying, the state of affairs created unilaterally in Poland by the USSR.

The following day, February 8, the British and Americans suggested replacing the word "enlarge," which made the provisional government in Warsaw the founder of the successor government, by words such as "establish" or "form." The Americans stood by their suggestions of a Presidential Polish Committee to intervene between the Warsaw government and the noncommunist Polish leaders. Churchill stated that in the absence of an agreement on Poland, the conference would be seen by the whole world as a "failure." Stalin refused to give up the Warsaw government. Roosevelt asked how soon elections could be held in Poland. "One month," Stalin replied, "unless there should

16. Roosevelt passed a piece of paper to Hopkins on which he had scribbled "This is not so good," in *The Conferences at Malta and Yalta,* 712.

be an unexpected catastrophe." The session ended soon thereafter.

We do not know whether Stalin's little comment had any effect. But on that same evening, Roosevelt drafted a fresh proposal with Stettinius, his secretary of state. On Friday, February 9, Stettinius arrived at the foreign ministers' meeting with the new text. The Americans had abandoned the idea of the Presidential Committee charged with "forming" a new government. They suggested that the actual provisional government, the one in Warsaw, should be "reorganized, *so as to* become fully representative."[17] Eden, taken by surprise, expressed his disagreement. Molotov, far from approving the American draft, insisted that continuity should be maintained between the Warsaw government and the one which was to be "reorganized." The final text, approved on February 10, foresaw a "reorganization" of the Warsaw provisional government under the auspices of a commission of the Three "to be held in Moscow and charged with drawing up the list of Poles who might participate in the reorganized government,"[18] which a few lines later was called "the new provisional government." It was to hold elections under universal suffrage. But it proved impossible to get the Soviets to accept any form of international supervision of these elections. Such supervision, Molotov said, would hurt the self-esteem of the Poles! The compromise reached with so much difficulty concerned the most important question for the USSR. It was clearly weighted in favor of the Soviet position and it was basically due to Roosevelt.

17. "That the Polish Provisional Government be reorganized [as a] fully representative government," ibid., 816.

18. According to the English text, the commission must "consult, first in Moscow, members of the provisional government and other democratic leaders from Poland or from other countries." According to the Russian text, it must "consult, first in Moscow, the members of the provisional government and other leaders, etc."

Yugoslavia

The compromise on Yugoslavia was of the same nature, although it was on the whole favored by the British. The Tito-Šubašić agreement was disavowed by King Peter II (in fact it conceded preponderance to Tito). The British, who nonetheless backed this agreement, insisted that two modest requests emanating from London should be met: (1) the representative assembly of the Resistance (AVNOJ) was to be completed after the liberation with members of the old Parliament who had not collaborated with the enemy, and (2) the legislative acts adopted by the AVNOJ were to be subject to confirmation after the war by the Parliament.

These recommendations were to have little effect. The new government was to consist of twenty-one members nominated by Tito and six by Šubašić. In Stalin's last message to Roosevelt on April 7, concerning Poland, Stalin proposed that the Polish government should be similarly made up.[19] Thus one discovers Stalin's long-term plan: in friendly countries—Poland, Czechoslovakia, and Yugoslavia—governments would be under communist control; in the conquered countries—Romania, Bulgaria, and Hungary—the formula was the same, but it was to be unilaterally imposed by the Soviet commander-in-chief. Between the principles proclaimed at Yalta and the Soviet reality was a hiatus that could not be bridged.

Liberated Europe

The declaration on a liberated Europe, also adopted on February 10, was obviously incapable of restoring the balance. The goal of this text of American origin was to recall the principles of the Atlantic Charter. It foresaw, in

19. M. J. Herz, *Beginnings of the Cold War* (New York: McGraw-Hill, 1969), 92.

general terms, the reestablishment of the basic freedoms in the liberated countries of Europe with the assistance of the Three Powers (which France was invited to join).

But Roosevelt turned down the idea put forward by the State Department to establish an Emergency European Commission charged with helping to restore democratic institutions in the liberated countries. At the request of the Soviets, the declaration, which was drafted in very general terms, was further weakened by the fact that only consultations among the Four were foreseen in emergencies, but there would be no organization, let alone power, to take action. The zone in which Soviet influence was already paramount thus remained sheltered from any liberal influence, whereas in the west strong Communist parties constituted powerful means of action for the USSR. Moreover, since the British and the Americans had not obtained any improvement in the status of their representatives on the Armistice Commission in Romania, Bulgaria, and Hungary (where they had been reduced to the level of tacit observers), the principal difficulty of the immediate postwar period began to emerge: in the zone under its control, the USSR exerted *exclusive* influence without any sharing; in the Western zone it impinged on opinion by many methods, especially in Italy, Belgium, and France, and it could make its voice heard. The game was not fair.

The game was not fair because people in the west did not yet know that this was the case. This is shown by the negotiations between Stalin and Roosevelt over the Far East.

These were conversations rather than negotiations. In two short sessions on February 8 and 10, Roosevelt approved all of Stalin's demands: the southern part of the island of Sakhalin and the Kurile Islands (a list of which had not even been drawn up) were to be taken from Japan. The USSR was to dispose of two ports in Chinese territory, Dairen and Port Arthur. It was to control the East China and South Manchurian railroads. The Nationalist Chinese government was to confirm the status of the People's Republic of China, that is to say the protectorate exercised by the USSR over this republic. In return for this, Stalin undertook open hostilities against Japan three months after the Armistice in Europe and also concluded a "treaty of friendship and alliance" with the nationalist Chinese government, against which the Chinese communists were fighting.

Strange conversations indeed! One side claimed its reward. The other accepted all the demands submitted to it. But the one which was going to have to satisfy some of them was an ally of the United States, Kuomintang China. Was it not possible to maintain certain reservations while accepting to act as a go-between with the Chinese nationalist government? How does one win respect? By accepting everything or by differentiating between sacrifices imposed on the enemy and those asked of an ally?

The Outcome

If we assess the outcome of the Yalta negotiations, we find that in *Europe* the Soviet Union obtained most of what it wanted: in *Poland* the government, imported from the USSR and rejected by that country, was to be "reorganized," that is to say "enlarged" as the USSR had proposed during the crucial session of February 7.[20] However, we also note that more than four months of increasingly tense negotiations would be needed before Stalin obtained the essentials of what he wanted in this field. In *Yugoslavia,* Tito was on his way to the rapid elimination of his enemies, as was Dimitrov in Bulgaria. The fate of Czechoslovakia and Hungary remained hanging in the balance. In *Germany,* the

20. See above, 75–76.

USSR did not win its allies over to its claim of $10 billion, demanded under the heading of reparations. Roosevelt accepted the figure as a "basis for discussion," Churchill refused to commit himself. The facts remained that Germany was to be occupied, that it would not have a national government, and that the principle of unanimity of the four victors who assumed the supreme power in Germany constituted a powerful lever for the USSR, whether to impose its views or to isolate its zone. If the United States were only to keep its forces in Europe for a short time, Great Britain, in order to contain a Soviet thrust, could look only to the western and Mediterranean fringes of Europe. The outcome would run the risk of being decided under extremely unequal conditions.

In *East Asia,* Stalin got from Roosevelt everything he asked for. In exchange, he abandoned the inordinate demands he had made in regard to the *United Nations,* which, in any case, he would not have been able to maintain, faced by the reaction of the vast majority of the countries which had participated in the creation of the organization. Thus, all things considered, he won. But what exactly did he win?

He extended his influence up to the Elbe and beyond as far as the approaches to the North Sea and the Adriatic. But was this influence sound and secure? Was it, as the Soviet press claims to this day, the result of an agreement that fixed specific zones of influence, a partition? Not at all. No text, no agreement (even implicit) provided for Marxism-Leninism to rule in the east, and liberal democracy in the west. At Yalta, the Allies were no doubt not firm enough. This does not mean that they subscribed in advance to the abuses which created strong tensions as early as 1945 in the Soviet-occupied territories and led to two ruptures: between the West and the USSR from 1947 on, and between communist Yugoslavia and the communist regime in Moscow in 1948. Thus one cannot agree with General de Gaulle's thesis in his *Mémoires:* "The huge portion of Europe which the Yalta agreements handed over in advance to the Soviets now lay in their hands."[21] The territories indeed lay "in their hands," but between February 1945 and the spring of 1947, the negotiations between the Four Powers (the United States, Great Britain, France, and the Soviet Union) addressed the means of putting an end to the situation that resulted from the war in order to achieve a form of peace which implied self-determination for the states to the east of the line of demarcation. It was not a matter of giving up anything, but of a setback. Hence the Cold War which emerged after 1945, a situation which has not evolved in forty-three years and has not consolidated itself correspondingly.

Why? Because, to the surprise of many people, exclusive influence exercised in one country by the armed forces of another country generates internal and external tensions which themselves preclude a return to peace. If indeed influences of the East and West are free to cross or become intertwined, it is possible to envisage an international system, more or less in equilibrium, providing a certain degree of flexibility and avoiding intolerable tensions. In the opposite situation, one heads toward a dead end, crises, and absence of peace. The choice is either tolerance or confrontation!

Such were the problematics of Yalta and not a so-called partition, which neither side was prepared to contemplate. One side thought it could, when the time was ripe, continue to advance westward; the other wanted to establish normal relations with the countries to the east. Hence the paralysis, the efforts to remedy it, the successive negotiations without result up until 1947–1949, failure, the death of Stalin, the renewal of negotiations, the two Berlin

21. Charles de Gaulle, *Mémoires de guerre*, vol. 3 (Paris: Plon, 1959), 202.

crises (1948–1949 and 1958–1962), the fearsome Cuban crisis, and the rest.

All of this stemmed not from Yalta but to a large extent from the nature of the Soviet system itself. How else can one explain the crises within the alliance which followed Yalta between February and June 1945?

6
The Crisis
(February–August 1945)

Immediately following the Yalta agreements, a crisis occured between the USSR and its partners after the victorious conclusion of the war, which turned into a basic disagreement and was to lead, from June 1947 on, to the break between the Soviet Union and the Western powers and to the Berlin blockade one year later.

Why this turnabout? Why did it persist over several decades? People usually answer the first question by invoking the unraveling of coalitions as soon as a common enemy is no longer there. But one cannot conclude that permanent confrontation necessarily flows from the emergence of differences. People reply to the second question with the argument of the basic incompatibility between socialism and capitalism or the inevitable rivalry between the two most powerful states. But capitalism and socialism are abstract entities that cannot explain much. As for inevitable rivalry between two powerful states, this is a possibility, not a necessity. How could it explain the crisis which broke out suddenly, and has lasted over several decades? Misunderstandings and dissensions are always possible. A radical dissension lasting more than forty years must have had specific causes whose origin should be identified.

We have seen that a conference is like a battle: a breakthrough occurs, an attempt is made to seal the breach, and finally, the situation is assessed. No one has entirely won or lost. But one has gained more than the others. Everyone knows what the real situation is even though people don't talk about it. Stalin certainly didn't win everything at Yalta, but he did manage to win acceptance of priority of his rights over Poland. This was no trifle, and he was to draw certain conclusions from it.

People often say that the British and the Americans left Yalta convinced that a cloudless future lay before them. This may have been true for Hopkins, Roosevelt's adviser, and for the president or the prime minister during the final toasts. But when we read their speeches after their return home, we note that behind the reassuring words there lurk doubts, not to say worries.

In the House of Commons on February 27, 1945, Churchill gave a positive assessment of the conference. But, while expressing pleasure over the agreements concerning Poland, he asked himself some questions:

> Are they [the Poles] to be free, as we in Britain and the United States or France are free? Are their sovereignty and their independence to be untrammelled, or are they to become a mere projection of the Soviet State? . . . We are now entering a world of imponderables. . . . It is a mistake to look too far ahead. . . . The ties that bind the three Great Powers together and their mutual comprehension of each other have grown. The United States has entered deeply and constructively into the life and salvation of Europe. We have all three set our hands to

far-reaching engagements at once practical and solemn.[1]

Two days later, before the U.S. Congress, Roosevelt, tired and emaciated, also betrayed some uncertainty in spite of the positive tone of his speech: "Twenty-five years ago," he said in conclusion, "American fighting men looked to the statesmen of the world to finish the work of peace for which they fought and suffered. We failed—we failed them then. We cannot fail them again, and expect the world to survive again."[2]

These were not empty words. Two weeks after the Yalta communiqué, Andrei Vyshinsky, deputy minister of foreign affairs, arrived in Bucharest, where trouble had broken out. He ordered King Michael to replace General Radesco as head of the government with an obscure progressive, M. Groza, leader of the Farmers' Front. The king yielded. Thus the Declaration on Liberated Europe, which provided for consultations between the Allies in the event of trouble, applied neither to Romania nor to the neighboring countries where members of noncommunist parties were threatened, hounded, and arrested. As Soviet historian Mileïkovski wrote, "The Soviet Union, while refraining from any intervention in the internal affairs of the liberated countries, did not tolerate any attack on their sovereignty on the part of other states."

As a result, England and the United States were unable "to impose reactionary governments on these countries."[3]

1. W. Churchill, *The Second World War,* vol. 6 (Boston: Houghton Mifflin, 1950), 400–401.

2. J. M. Burns, *Roosevelt, the Soldier of Freedom* (London: Weidenfeld and Nicolson, 1971), 582.

3. *International Relations after the Second World War,* vol. 1 (in Russian) (Moscow, 1962), 31.

Poland

The crisis over Poland was graver still. As soon as the commission, agreed to in Yalta in order to prepare the "reorganization" of the provisional government, met in Moscow, a dispute surfaced which had not been settled before Roosevelt's death. According to Molotov, the Polish political nominees to be convoked by the commission must first satisfy two conditions: their support of the Yalta agreements and the concurrence of the provisional Warsaw government. The messages that Churchill and Roosevelt sent to Stalin had no effect. The Russian text of the Yalta agreements did not say the same thing as the English text.[4] At the end of March, the Soviet government, without having consulted its allies, placed the German provinces lying to the east of the Oder and the western Neisse under Polish administration, thereby disposing, by unilateral action, of territories subject to the collective authority of the victors. At about the same time in Poland, sixteen leaders of the Polish Resistance, who had been invited to meet with Soviet authorities, found themselves imprisoned in Moscow, accused of sabotage and anti-Soviet activities. Also at the end of March, Moscow announced that Molotov would not be able to attend the San Francisco conference at which, in accordance with the Yalta agreement, the future charter of the United Nations was to be worked out.

On April 21, 1945, the Warsaw provisional government, which had been neither reorganized nor recognized, concluded with the USSR an assistance pact whose clauses were very close to the pacts with Czechoslovakia and France.[5] A similar pact was concluded as early as April 11 by the USSR with Yugoslavia.

4. See Chapt. 5, 77, n. 18.

5. See Chapt. 4, 55–58.

The only explanation one can find for this policy, so harmful to the interests of the party pursuing it, is based on the premise that Stalin hastened to consolidate his gains before the end of hostilities. The better to cover himself, he accused the British and the Americans, during the entire month of March and up until the death of Roosevelt, of negotiating the surrender of the German forces in northern Italy separately with the Germans in order, he said, to permit the Wehrmacht to concentrate all its resources on the eastern front. This is what is known as the "Bern incident." It merits some attention.

The Bern Incident

Allen Dulles, the brother of John Foster Dulles, was the representative in Bern of the OSS, Office of Strategic Studies, which might also be called the Office of Secret Services.[6] In this capacity he was informed in late February 1945 that the German forces in northern Italy were prepared to surrender. An initial contact was planned in Bern, after which discussions were to continue at General Alexander's headquarters at Caserta. The Soviet government was informed on March 12. Molotov replied on the same day: no objection, but on condition that representatives of the Soviet High Command participate in the Bern conversation.

As it was a matter of preliminary and secret contacts with a view to discussions to be held at Caserta, both the American ambassador to Moscow and the heads of the Combined Chiefs of Staff in Washington felt that a Soviet presence, while acceptable at Caserta, would serve no useful purpose in Bern, where moreover it would risk drawing

6. Here we follow the account given by H. Feis in his book *Churchill, Roosevelt, Stalin* (Princeton, N.J.: Princeton University Press, 1957), 583–595.

attention to its presence and thereby wreck the whole project. Molotov was informed on the 15th and replied on the 16th with a very tough letter: the Soviet government could not give its concurrence (Molotov had written "its agreement"[7]) to the talks in Bern. The Western Allies refused to interrupt the contact with the Germans and the quarrel gradually became more acrimonious. Roosevelt wrote to Stalin, who replied. The latter declared himself convinced, on the basis of his informers, that negotiations (with the Germans) had taken place and that they had resulted in an agreement according to which Marshal Kesselring, commander-in-chief on the western front, accepted to open the front and to let the Anglo-American forces advance eastward, his enemies having promised in return to make the terms of the surrender much more lenient. Roosevelt replied on April 5 with an indignant letter.

> Finally I would say this; it would be one of the great tragedies of history if, at the very moment of the victory now within our grasp, such distrust, such lack of faith should prejudice the entire undertaking after the colossal losses of life, material and treasure involved.
>
> Frankly, I cannot avoid a feeling of bitter resentment toward your informers, whoever they are, for such vile misrepresentations of my actions or those of my trusted subordinates.[8]

Stalin replied on April 7: he stuck to his position, but let it be understood that he had not intended to offend anyone. On April 11, Roosevelt sent Churchill a brief message: "I would minimize the general Soviet problem as

7. SAMOT, 2:332.

8. *The Secret History of World War II, The Ultra-Secret Wartime Letters and Cables of Roosevelt, Stalin, and Churchill* (New York: Richardson & Steirman, 1986), 265–266.

much as possible because these problems, in one form or another, seem to arise every day and most of them straighten out as in the case of the Bern meeting. We must be firm, however, and our course thus far is correct."[9]

On the following day, April 12, Roosevelt died suddenly. As for the preliminary contacts in Bern, they came to nothing.

What is one to think of this strange episode? We can guess the motives if we recall the discussion at Yalta about dismembering Germany.[10] Stalin had not forgotten the dirty trick he played on the western powers at the time of the nonaggression pact of August 23, 1939. How could the latter refrain from paying him back in his own coin when the occasion arose? He tried to forestall them by suggesting that the threat of the dismemberment of Germany be included in the act of surrender. He did not succeed. The danger of collusion between the enemy and the Western Allies arose concretely, so he thought, in March. Therefore one must scare them. Taking into account Stalin's character, his guile, and his conviction that there were more affinities than hostility between his allies and the enemy, one glimpses the reasons for an attitude which the toughest of leaders would doubtless have avoided when only a few weeks from victory. Here, Stalin was not inspired by Marxism-Leninism so much as by his atavism: too sly for his own intelligence. "Stalin," one of his future victims used to say, "Stalin is a bandit. This bandit has a bandit's concept of Marxism. That's all!"[11] Now that the nightmare of this war

9. Francis Loewenheim and Harold D. Langley, *Roosevelt and Churchill, Their Secret Wartime Correspondence* (New York, E. P. Dutton & Co., Inc., 1975), 709.

10. See Chapt. 5, 70–74.

11. The person in question is Yuri Steklov, editor-in-chief of *Izvestia*, during an aside in the Kremlin in December 1925 with N. Valentinov. Steklov was to die in a concentration camp. Cf. N. Valentinov, *Nep i Krizis Partii* (Stanford: Hoover Institution Press, 1971), 251.

was on the point of coming to an end, Stalin saw in his allies or partners only his own reflection.

The seizure of countries between the USSR and Germany (not to say the west) went forward actively. In Poland, the fight against noncommunist parties was intensified. In Yugoslavia, where Tito, in spite of the agreements he had reached with the royal government-in-exile set up a purely communist regime, the ardor of the partisans led to strong tension with the British. The latter nevertheless succeeded in establishing in Istria, in May, a line of demarcation which left Trieste to Italy. During this period, American policy betrayed a kind of hesitation which manifested itself in two contradictory episodes: early in 1945, the United States failed to reply to a Soviet request for a $6 billion credit for postwar reconstruction and in May–June 1945, Harry Hopkins, sent to Moscow by Truman, gave the USSR everything it had demanded concerning Poland.

The American Credit to the USSR

From July 21, 1941, until the end of the hostilities, the USSR received all kinds of merchandise under Lend-Lease for a total value of $9.5 billion, about 20 percent of the total deliveries to U.S. allies. These deliveries consisted of 14,700 planes; 7,000 tanks; 52,000 jeeps; 376,000 trucks; 35,000 motorcycles; 11,000 freight cars; 3,800,000 tires; 15,000,000 pairs of boots; etc.[12] One-third of the total sum served to finance civilian equipment required for the reconstruction of the Soviet industrial machine. The nearer to the end of the war, the more the Soviet representatives took an interest in deliveries relating to the civilian economy (factories, machine tools, etc.) and the more-responsible

12. M. F. Herz, *Beginnings of the Cold War* (New York: McGraw-Hill, 1969), 159 (from the 21st Report to Congress on operations under the title of Lend-Lease).

American personnel had to be mindful of Congress, which insisted on observing a clear distinction between furnishing armaments or military equipment on the one hand and tools destined for reconstruction on the other.

In the fall of 1944 John Winant, the American ambassador in London, sent a report to Washington stressing that if one wished to help the USSR, one should plan a policy for the postwar period based simultaneously on reparations imposed on Germany and American aid, which "should be tied to a satisfactory settlement of the German reparations problem as well as to the principal outstanding political questions between the two governments."[13] The analysis was sound, but the report itself seems to have vanished in the administrative maze. Closely argued discussions were indeed being held in order to fix the total and the nature of deliveries to the Soviet Union under Lend-Lease for the fiscal year 1944–1945. The rate of interest was argued inch by inch: each side stuck to its position.

On January 3, 1945, Molotov handed Averell Harriman, the U.S. ambassador, a memorandum on the grant by the United States to the USSR of a credit of $6 billion for postwar reconstruction. The text, so drafted as to suggest that it was a matter of helping the United States reconvert its industry and avoid unemployment, might have served as the starting point for thorough discussion. But it seems that for symmetrical reasons (one side not wanting to beg, the other wishing to keep its distance) neither the soliciting nor the solicited government was disposed to initiate the discussion. At Yalta, Molotov said a word about this credit to Stettinius. Stettinius said he was ready to discuss it. This was how things remained. After Yalta, negotiations on the Lend-Lease program (concerned to a considerable extent with material destined for reconstruction) were unsuccessful. Neither of the two partners considered himself to be in

13. Ibid., 165.

a position to make concessions on the rate of interest. Above all, events subsequent to Yalta turned the United States away from a policy of aid to the USSR without compensations. And how could these be obtained when in eastern Europe, the *faits accomplis* were multiplying and Soviet officials in Germany were carrying out a policy of unilateral dismantling, the total value of which no one could compute? "When the matter involves their security," wrote Charles E. Bohlen in 1944, "the Soviet leaders see no conflict between a policy of cooperation on a world level and a policy of unilateral action in areas of direct interest to them."[14]

As a result, the Soviet request for credits remained unanswered. The United States thereby deprived themselves of an instrument permitting them to affect Soviet policy in Europe, an instrument which would, in any case, have been very difficult to use. As for the Soviet Union, it kept its hands free. Had the $6 billion credit been granted in 1946, could the Soviet Union in 1947 have denounced the Marshall plan as an enterprise of imperialist domination? Nevertheless, Truman, under Harriman's advice, was still trying to restore communications with the USSR. In June 1945, he sent Harry Hopkins to Moscow to try to find a way out of the Polish deadlock.

The Hopkins Mission to Moscow
(May 25–June 9, 1945)

In Moscow, where Hopkins spent two weeks, the dead ends were the same as at Yalta:[15] no progress in Poland

---

14. C. E. Bohlen, "Memorandum, May 6, 1944" (National Archives, Washington, D.C.). Translator's note: I was unable to locate this memorandum.

15. We note that on April 12, Stalin, receiving Harriman on the evening of Roosevelt's death, agreed to reexamine the decision not to send Molotov to San Francisco.

short of prior acceptance of the Soviet thesis on the "enlargement" of the provisional government and disagreement on the right of veto in the U.N. Security Council: in San Francisco, Molotov once again requested that unanimity of the Big Five be required even for procedural decisions (in particular for inscription of a question on the Council's agenda). In the course of several conversations, Hopkins, rising above diplomatic bargaining, tried to convince Stalin that the crisis was serious: American opinion was disturbed, one could not continue like this. But he insisted that the United States wanted the Polish government to be friendly toward the USSR. In reply, Stalin enumerated relatively minor grievances: the abrupt interruption of deliveries under Lend-Lease as of May 11 (canceled a few days later by Truman); the isolation of the Soviet delegation in certain discussions at the San Francisco Conference; the admission of France to the Reparations Commission created at Yalta (an "insult" to the USSR, which had fought so well, whereas France had surrendered in 1940); lack of a reply to the Soviet request that it be awarded part of the German battle fleet; and finally, of course, Poland: the government in power was very popular, all that needed to be done was to include four new members (out of twenty-one). It will be noted that Stalin did not include the lack of a reply to his request for a $6 billion credit in his list of grievances.

Hopkins pleaded Poland's case ably. But, captive of the idea that this Poland must be the "friend" of the USSR (whereas, after what had happened between 1939 and 1941, it was the USSR which should be trying to win the "friendship" of Poland), he was gradually brought around to giving ground and finally to accepting enlargement as Stalin had foreseen it: four noncommunist ministers (among whom was Mikolajczyk) in a government in which the communists were in the majority. Stalin was disposed to support the national government in China, that of

Chiang Kai-shek; he gave up insisting on unanimity among the Five in the Security Council for drafting the agenda— concessions which didn't cost him much. On the other hand, when Hopkins intervened in favor of the sixteen leaders of the Polish Resistance, imprisoned in Moscow as the result of an ambush, he ran into a stone wall: the trial must be held. It was in fact held in Moscow; several of those condemned were later to die in prison. Stalin had won Poland and the United States obtained his agreement to a July meeting of the Big Three in Potsdam. The scales were not evenly weighted.

The Potsdam Conference
(July 17–August 2, 1945)

Not only did the conference held in Potsdam fail to heal the split in Europe, as it appeared in the spring of 1945, but it revealed the scale of Soviet designs in relation to the world and primarily to Germany.

Significant in this respect was the haste with which the Soviets organized the zone which had been assigned to it. By June 9, 1945, the Soviet Military Administration for Germany had already been put in place. On the following day, Ordinance No. 2 authorized "the creation and activity in the Soviet zone of all antifascist parties . . . under the control of the Soviet military administration and in conformity with its instructions."[16] This ordinance came as a surprise to the German communists: the project, prepared in the USSR during the war, foresaw a great antifascist movement, the "bloc of fighting democracy" grouping together all men of goodwill. And now, suddenly, in June, not only was there a return to political parties, but opposition

16. H. Weber, *Von der SBZ zur DDR*, vol. 1 (Hanover: Verlag für Literatur and Zeitgeschehen, 1966), 16.

to a merger between the Socialist and Communist parties. This note of caution seems to find its explanation in a long-term plan affecting the western zones, which emerged when Molotov proposed at Potsdam the immediate creation in Berlin of a certain number of "central German administrations." As early as July 27, 1945, eleven central German administrations had been created in the Soviet zone of Germany, whose role was confined to the zone, but which suggested "matrix cells" of a central German government.[17] Having in mind a probable withdrawal of the Americans, it was not absurd to prepare in Berlin the cadres of the future German state. If the USSR showed itself bent on the subjugation of Poland, an allied country, it should not seem to it impossible also to subjugate Germany, a conquered country, in which it enjoyed a permanent right of intervention. As Walter Ulbricht said, on his return from the USSR in order to reestablish the German Communist Party (KPD), "It must look democratic, but everything must be controlled by us."[18]

Thus we understand why the Potsdam Conference could only confirm the state of affairs resulting from the war. Churchill's and Truman's protestations against the Soviet seizure of the eastern countries, against the unilateral definition of the Polish frontier on the Oder-Neisse line, and against the exactions of all kinds carried out by the USSR in its zone under the heading of reparations, came up against the hard facts: the Soviet zone, the Oder-Neisse line, and the governments with a communist majority.

It was under these conditions, while the conference was suspended for a few days pending the outcome of the English elections, that U.S. Secretary of State James F.

17. Ibid., 22.

18. W. Leonhard, *Die Revolution entlässt Ihre Kinder* (Cologne: Kiepenheuer and Witsch, 1955), 358.

Byrnes, a former senator, thought up the compromise which would permit everyone to go home again.

1. Reparations were to be levied by each of the victors in his zone. The USSR was to receive (in return for deliveries of foodstuffs from the eastern zone to the western zones) 25 percent of the industrial equipment destined to be dismantled in the west. But what would remain of German unity?

2. The Oder-Neisse line was accepted as the provisional Polish frontier with Germany, "subject to the peace treaty." But that "provisional" was very likely to prove definitive.

3. The preparation of peace treaties with the former German allies was to be speeded up so that by the end of these negotiations normal diplomatic relations could be established between the western powers and the governments under consideration. In the meantime, members of the English and American missions in the eastern countries were to enjoy greater freedom of movement than hitherto. But communist preponderance was to remain intact.

Thus ended the Potsdam meeting on August 2, 1945. Despite Mr. Byrnes's "compromise," the conference left behind bad memories with the English and American participants: the USSR had proposed quadripartite control of the Ruhr basin; it had stated its interest in a trusteeship for Libya; it had proposed to Turkey a bilateral agreement for the "common" defense of the Black Sea straits; and finally, while recommending collective condemnation of General Franco's regime in Spain, it had expressed the desire to reoccupy the place intended for Russia on the international Administration of Tangiers. These proposals, particularly that aimed at the Ruhr, gave the impression that the Soviet Union had long-term plans and that these extended far beyond the zone occupied by the Soviet forces.

From the Soviet viewpoint, the Yalta and Potsdam conferences could be summarized in two words: *Poland* and

Germany. At Yalta, Stalin swiped Poland. At Potsdam he attempted to install a plan of action aimed at the whole of Germany.[19] Had this second operation succeeded, the whole of Europe would have found itself under the "protection" of the USSR.

In 1945, Stalin had no thought of partitioning. Partitioning would have meant a western Europe free of all Soviet influence. Neither at Yalta nor in any of the war or postwar negotiations was there any question of such a division and the only agreement which mentioned it was that concerning the Balkans which Churchill and Stalin sketched out in October 1944: Greece under British influence, Romania and Bulgaria under that of the USSR, and Yugoslavia and Hungary under joint influence. But this agreement remained very much up in the air, with the USSR tightening its hold on eastern and central Europe and Greece only escaping communist domination after a four-year civil war.

Thus Yalta was only one moment in an evolution that, even today, may not have run its course. If we wish to express a soundly based opinion on this conference, we must, after recalling the principal criticisms it has aroused, ask ourselves two questions. Could we have done better? Can something be done today to break the deadlock?

19. Referring to the "bloc of antifascist parties," created in the Soviet zone on July 14, 1945, Colonel Tulpanov, who played an important role in the Soviet zone, writes, "The Soviet military administration considered the bloc [of antifascist parties] as an organism whose decisions concerned not only the [Soviet] zone, but all the zones, since its authority stemmed from the decisions at Potsdam" (S. Tulpanov, "Die Rolle der SMAD bei der Demokratisierung Deutschlands," in *Zeitschrift für Geschichtswissenschaft,* Berlin-Est, 1967, No. 2, 248).

7
Yesterday, Today, Tomorrow

At first reading, the final communiqué of Yalta appeared to reflect complete understanding between the Three: *Germany,* after her defeat, was to be not only controlled but governed by the victors, disarmed, reeducated, and democratized; and was to make reparations for the damages she had caused. An international conference was to draft the Charter of the United Nations, the worldwide organization which would keep the United States from withdrawing within itself once again, and permit the USSR to cooperate with the noncommunist world. The *liberated European countries* would receive help from the Three, if needed, for the establishment of democratic institutions and representative governments. In *Poland,* a coalition would be created which would pledge itself to organize free elections as soon as possible. In *Yugoslavia,* the legislative measures decreed by the resistance would have to be ratified by a Constituent Assembly. *France* was to occupy a zone in Germany and be a member of the Control Council in Berlin. Finally, a Council of Ministers of Foreign Affairs would meet regularly in order to maintain a close exchange of views between governments. Who would disapprove of such a program?

In the United States and Great Britain, the first press comments were positive.

"Even the first glance," *The New York Times* reported on February 13, 1945, "gives assurance that, though they may disappoint some individual expectations, they justify and surpass most of the hopes placed on this fateful meeting. . . . They point the way to an early victory in Europe, to a secure peace, and to a brighter world."

The *London Times* reported, on the same date, that "This time, the Gordian knot has been cut. Another crisis within the Polish government is inevitable, but people are convinced that all reasonable Poles finally will live with the agreement reached."

The Soviet press insisted particularly on the strengthening of *unity* among the Allies. What unity? In its February 13th issue, *Izvestia* reported that "the solutions envisaged for Poland and Yugoslavia indicate how the declaration on a liberated Europe will be carried out in practice." These are more than mere reservations.

The French press showed caution. In *Le Figaro* on February 15, Wladimir d'Ormesson applauded the compromises on Poland and Yugoslavia. "We shall judge these formulas of agreement by the manner in which they are carried out." He urged the French not to indulge in "bitterness." "France has again found allies between whom she draws no distinction." On February 25, under the same signature, *Le Figaro* considered the declaration on a liberated Europe "a convergence of points of view, a strengthening of common Anglo-Soviet-American action."

The editorials of *Le Monde* (February 15 and 21) are even more restrained. The agreement on Poland signifies a concession by the USSR, "at least in appearance." Mikolajczyk was to be invited to Moscow by the Commission of the Three. One must hope for his success "without believing in it too much." The Yalta agreements arouse "very lively but incomplete" satisfaction. Finally, the newspaper

asks what is to be France's role in the United Nations. Will
France be represented at the meetings of the ministers of
foreign affairs?[1]

Criticisms of Polish origin, or emanating from circles
close to the Polish leaders were the sharpest. In the United
States, Senator Vandenberg considered the agreement on
Poland "very bad." In London, during the parliamentary
debate, twenty-five members of the majority voted against
the government, eleven others abstained.

The dilemma in which Churchill and Roosevelt found
themselves is revealed in letters exchanged on the eve of
the conference between two American experts, both future
ambassadors in Moscow, George F. Kennan and Charles E.
Bohlen. Kennan had been counselor of the U.S. Embassy
in Moscow since July 1944; for several months, Bohlen was
the special assistant to the secretary of state (charged with
liaison with the White House). On February 4, 1945, Kennan sent Bohlen, who was arriving at Yalta with the American delegation, a very stern letter on the policy of the
Western Allies.

> I am aware of the realities of this war, and of the
> fact that we are too weak to win it without Russian
> cooperation. I recognize that Russia's war effort has
> been masterful and effective and must, to a certain
> extent, find its reward at the expense of other
> peoples in eastern and central Europe.
>
> But with all of this, I fail to see why we must

1. In February 1945, General de Gaulle had not publicly expressed his
opinion on the Yalta agreements. It was after 1947 when, in order to launch the
Rassemblement du peuple français, he took a very critical position in regard to commu-
nism and thus the Soviet Union, that he denounced the "policy of blocs," which
he considered to be that of Yalta. The same opinions appear in his *Mémoires de
guerre* (vol. 3, Paris: Plon, 1959, 80, 90, 202) as well as, twenty-three years later,
in the French communiqué of August 21, 1968: "The armed intervention of the
Soviet Union in Czechoslovakia shows that the Moscow government has not freed
itself from the policy of blocs imposed on Europe by Yalta."

associate ourselves with this political program, so
hostile to the interests of the Atlantic community
as a whole, so dangerous to everything which we
need to see preserved in Europe. Why could we not
make a decent and definitive compromise with it—
divide Europe frankly into spheres of influence—
keep ourselves out of the Russian sphere and
keep the Russians out of ours? That would have
been the best thing we could do for ourselves
and for our friends in Europe, and the most
honest approach we could have tried to restore
life, in the wake of war, on a dignified and stable
foundation.

Instead of this . . . we have refused to name
any limit for Russian expansion and Russian
responsibilities, thereby confusing the Russians and
causing them constantly to wonder whether they are
asking too little or whether it was some kind of a
trap.[2]

Kennan made four specific suggestions:

1. That plans for the United Nations be buried
   . . . because [they] would . . . commit the United
   States to defend a . . . "Russian Sphere of
   power."
2. That . . . the United States must reserve to itself
   the right to decide where to use armed force.
3. That the United States should write off Eastern
   and Southeastern Europe unless it possessed the
   will [to] oppose with all its physical and
   diplomatic resources Russian domination of the
   area.
4. That the United States . . . begin consultations

2. Bohlen, *Witness to History* (New York: Norton & Co., 1973), 175.

with the British and French about the formation
of a Western European federation which would
include West German states.[3]

Behind these proposals, one discerns the seeds of the
policy of resistance ("containment") advocated by Kennan
from 1947 on. One also sees that no American leader could
have followed this road in 1945 without forfeiting the support of public opinion.

That is what Charles Bohlen wrote in his reply:

As you know, there is a great deal in your
expositions that I agree with. You should know that
in this connection the U.S. government is following
admittedly a policy of no small risk. But have you
ever seriously thought through the alternatives? The
"constructive" suggestions that you make are
frankly naive to a degree. They may well be the
optimum from an abstract point of view. But as
practical suggestions they are utterly impossible.
Foreign policy of that kind cannot be made in a
democracy. Only totalitarian states can make and
carry out such policies. Furthermore, I don't for
one minute believe that there has been any time in
this war when we could seriously have done very
differently than we did. It is easy to talk about
instruments of pressure that we had in our hands.
But the simple fact remains that if we wished to
defeat Germany we could never have even tried to
keep the Soviet armies out of Eastern Europe and
Germany itself. I can never figure out why a piece
of paper that you did not get should be regarded as
so much more real than those you did get. Isn't it a
question of realities and not bits of paper? Either

3. Ibid., 176.

our pals intend to limit themselves or they don't. I submit, as the British say, that the answer is not yet clear. But what is clear is that the Soyuz [Soviet Union] is here to stay, as one of the major factors in the world. Quarreling with them would be so easy, but we can always come to that.[4]

Thus, on the eve of the conference, two arguments confronted each other: *partition,* i.e., each remaining master in his own camp and the search for an *understanding,* i.e., no clean break, but *mutually intersecting* influences. The reality was otherwise; once the conference was over, it quickly appeared that partition, which had not been discussed at Yalta, would in any case be unfeasible: the Soviet system extended its antennas beyond the limits of its direct influence, liberal regimes had no access to areas under the control of the Soviet Union. Two weights, two measures!

From this state of affairs there emerged in 1949 in the United States the first wave of criticisms of the Yalta agreements, when Mao triumphed in China and Roosevelt's enemies accused the president retrospectively of incompetence and weakness. But on the whole, these criticisms did not call into question Washington's policy after the spring of 1947: support of Western Europe and the Atlantic Pact.

On the contrary, it was this policy that American "revisionist" historians denounced in the 1960s as imperialist, as having driven the Soviet Union to defend itself by isolating its "glacis" from all contact with the outside world.[5] These arguments aroused much attention at the time. They arouse few echoes today. In the USSR, on the other hand, the "imperialism" of the Western powers served from the

4. Ibid.

5. Cf. G. Kolko, *The Politics of War* (New York, 1950); G. Alperowitz, *Atomic Diplomacy* (London, 1966); D. Horowitz, *From Yalta to Vietnam* (New York, 1970); Fleming, *The Cold War and its Origins* (New York, 1961).

first to justify Soviet policy since the war. Seen from Moscow, the seizure of central and eastern Europe by the Soviet Union was the consequence of the evil designs of the West. "The American and British governments," Sipols and Tchelychev wrote, "sought to impose after the war their economic and political domination on Europe. They opposed the growing influence of the Soviet Union on the course of world events. In order to prevent any social transformation in the countries of Europe, they supported and reinforced reactionary regimes and movements."[6]

Similarly, in the *History of the Foreign Policy of the USSR:*

> The Soviet government considered that the new organs of power, as they emerged from the crucible of the national war of liberation, were representative of Poland. The positions of the United States and England were entirely different. These two countries sought to alter the composition of the new governments, not only in Poland, but in other liberated countries (including, for example France) in order to turn them into instruments of their policy."[7]

One sees that the partition of Europe (and of the world) was not the result of the Yalta agreements. The division stemmed from the nature of the Soviet system, from the way in which it had conceived itself since Lenin, Stalin, and their successors save, perhaps, two of them: Khrushchev (who nevertheless asserted that socialism "would bury" capitalism) and Gorbachev (whose long-term intentions we are not yet in a position to assess clearly). If this is so, we will be inclined to think that one could hardly

6. V. Sipols and I. Tchelychev, *Krymskaïa Konferentsia* (Moscow, 1984), 14.

7. Anatol A. Gromyko and B. N. Ponomarëv, *Istoriia Vnechneï politiki SSSR,* vol. 1 (Moscow: Nauka, 1976), 489.

have done better at Yalta. And yet, on looking closely, it
was possible to do something other than what Churchill
and Roosevelt did, especially Roosevelt.

Could One Have Done Better?

In an abstract sense, the answer is yes. One can always
do better. Practically speaking, we must recognize that in
February 1945 it was difficult to do better. Why? Because
from July 1941 until 1945, Stalin never met with any firm
opposition to his plans concerning Poland, even though
these made it possible to foretell the thrust of his policy,
both toward the Soviet Union's neighbors whether hostile
or friendly, as well as to Germany.

From 1941 to 1944, the lack of a second front paralyzed the Western leaders. They never dared to remind
Stalin that in May–June 1940 there was no second front in
eastern Europe, nor, above all, that from December 1941
on, the Pacific front was a second front protecting the
USSR from any Japanese threat to the Soviet far eastern
provinces. It is difficult to grasp just what it was that Roosevelt and Churchill feared. Probably they themselves would
not have been able to say. But in light of the precedent of
August 1939, the possibility of a low blow by Stalin could
not be entirely discounted. In his memoirs, Churchill re-
minds us that in wartime, one is not free to choose. "What
would have happened," he wrote, "if we had quarrelled
with Russia while the Germans still had three or four hundred divisions on the fighting front?"[8] This enables us to
explain up to a certain point the restraint shown toward
Stalin. Had he not written on August 1941, to Maiski, his
ambassador in London: "What do the English want? They
want us to be weakened. If this is so, let us be careful with

8. Churchill, *The Second World War,* vol. 6, 202.

the English!"[9] An alliance based on mutual distrust is not an alliance. Hence the extreme caution of the two western protagonists.

Granting this, the fact remains that we could have done a little better if restraint toward Stalin had been only one of the facets of a long-term policy. Without claiming to open up grandiose vistas to Stalin, we could have attempted to make him understand the advantages of an international security system based on a few principles, starting with the simplest; this principle could have been spelled out in specific terms: "If you want to have a friendly Poland, it is up to you to act in such a way that it can become your friend. For in September 1939, you were not one of its friends. Try to erase this stain! This will make it easier to settle the frontier problem." Western opinion could have brought its weight to bear in the right direction, while London and Washington would have attempted to arrive at a compromise, particularly on the frontier issue, acceptable to both sides, Poland and the Soviet Union. It is probable that such an initiative would have failed. But this failure, had it actually occurred, would have made it possible to have a better understanding of what the postwar period would be like. Stalin would have been faced with a choice: either moderation, especially in regard to Poland, and maintenance after the war of good relations between the major Allies, or the introduction of communist domination by force in Poland, in the Soviet zone of Germany, and in the whole of eastern Europe, and inescapable tension if not a break, with Great Britain and the United States. There might have ensued a different future from that which the European Allies of the USSR have known since 1945.

To act thus would have required a better understanding of the real nature of the war which started in 1939. It

9. Doc. no. 36 in *Sovetsko-Angliskie Otnocheniia (1941–1945)*, vol. 1 (Moscow, 1983), 109.

was a war against Hitlerian tyranny, not against Germany, a war which was to lead to peace based not only on a balance of forces and adjustment of "national interests," but on a certain degree of justice, that is to say, based on certain fundamental principles, short of which crises and conflicts would not fail to recur once the fighting was over.

On arriving at Yalta, Roosevelt, instead of declaring himself to be "bloodthirsty" would have done better to tell Stalin that he was hungry and thirsty for a real peace, that it was therefore necessary to achieve an equitable solution of the Polish problem, so to arrange matters that the Poles, all the Poles, should be treated properly. Far from speaking in this way, Roosevelt, and Churchill also, only too often spoke about the Polish government-in-exile as though it consisted of a few elderly gentlemen, at once retarded, obstinate, and utopian.[10] How, under these conditions, could Stalin, the wily and blasé Georgian, be persuaded to take into account the views of his allies, that is to say visualize, even in the distant future, the first outlines of a true peace? Not *peaceful coexistence,* which signifies the persistence of fundamental rivalry, but *peace,* that is to say, to start with, *tolerance* and if possible, one day, *mutual recognition.*

It has often been said that at Yalta Roosevelt and Churchill "betrayed" Europe. It is true that they could have shown themselves to be more clear-sighted. But so far as betraying goes, Europe betrayed itself long before Yalta: in July–August 1914 to start with, at Petrograd in October 1917, without any doubt at Versailles in June 1919; certainly in Berlin in January 1933; to some extent in London,

10. At the start of the fourth session at Yalta, on February 7, Roosevelt said that he "did not attach any importance to the continuity or legality of any Polish government because he thought in some years there had in reality been no Polish government" (in *Foreign Relations of the USA, The Conferences at Malta and Yalta,* Washington, D.C.: Government Printing Office, 1955, 709).

Paris, and Warsaw between the wars; and miserably at Vichy in 1940. No one can claim that he would have done much better on so ravaged a soil.

The question remains whether something can be done today or tomorrow.

Today and Tomorrow

Today there is something new in the air: "scientific socialism" inspired by Marx and applied by Lenin, seems to everyone to be not merely devoid of "scientific" character, but quite simply inefficient, incapable of fulfilling the promises of its great founders. Held in contempt by all the European countries into which it was forcibly introduced after 1945, it rapidly became simply tyranny in the underdeveloped countries, in which it managed to gain a foothold. In the Soviet Union, in China, in the eastern European countries, numerous currents of thought are arising, which cast doubt not only on the efficacy but on the validity of the regimes which had drawn their inspiration from Marx, Lenin, Mao, and others. These regimes in fact had in common the primacy of the party and the state over man, whereas reality is the reverse. The best part of a human being frees itself by its very nature from the constraints of the state or the party.

It can be said that this is well known. To which one can reply: more known than accepted, more accepted than applied. Nevertheless a step has been taken. In Gorbachev's USSR, as in today's China, attempts are being made to combine authority of the single party with individual or collective initiative, not only in the field of economics, but also in those of culture and information. Something has stirred. We don't know how long this will last, let alone what the outcome will be, but we do know that the way in which people now speak of Stalin in public meetings in Moscow is enough to make the bigwigs shiver.[11]

The important thing is not that the harshest criticisms may be aired, but that they should exist, and that they should be so pertinent. To be sure, the USSR of 1988 cannot be compared, for example, with Poland. But short of a "civilian society" which asserts its presence, we find in Russia elements of authentic civic conscience. No one knows what will come out of this quivering. But the very fact that it exists forces Western societies and their leaders to ask themselves a few questions on the policy to be followed during this period of uncertainty: can one attempt to influence opinions in the East and the West toward a state of affairs less far removed from peace than that in which we have been living for over forty years?

It is not a matter of again going over the text of the final act signed at Helsinki on August 1, 1975, which deals—in words at least—with "security and cooperation in Europe." This text, while on the whole satisfactory, was not followed by any results. Moreover, it tends to confirm the division of Germany and consequently, of the European continent. We must accurately assess the nature of the obstacles to be overcome.

The division of Germany has its origin in the unconditional surrender proclaimed by Roosevelt at Casablanca in January 1943. This surrender was much harsher than those imposed on Hitler's allies (Italy, Hungary, Romania, Bulgaria, and Finland). It provided for an initial period during which Germany was to be governed by the Allied Com-

---

11. To take only one example, we see in the weekly published in Paris, *La Pensée Russe* (Rousskaia Mysl), in the May 29, 1987, issue, the account of a public lecture on *"the excesses of Stalinism,"* delivered in Moscow on April 13, 1987. In the course of this meeting the most outspoken opinions were aired by numerous participants. A twenty-two-year-old archivist has estimated the number of those rehabilitated since Stalin's death at "612,500 dead or alive." Do not such "excesses" cause anyone to reflect on the shortcomings of the "single party"?

manders-in-Chief. The text prepared in London by the European Advisory Commission stipulated that "supreme authority in Germany shall be exercised, . . . by the British, United States, Soviet, and French Commanders-in-Chief, *each in his own zone of occupation,* and also jointly, in matters affecting Germany as a whole. The four Commanders-in-Chief will together constitute the Control Council." There can be unity only if the Four are in agreement. Under these conditions, how can division be avoided? Thought was given to this in Washington in the spring of 1945, and the American delegation at Potsdam presented a new text which gave the control council higher authority than each commander-in-chief. This proposal was turned down by the Soviets. The trend toward division carried the day. It became unavoidable when the French government, in the fall of 1945, opposed the creation of central administrations in Berlin.[12] From then on Germany was divided not into four, but into two: to the east, the Soviet zone; to the west, the three Western zones, out of which the Federal Republic of Germany was to emerge in 1949, facing the German Democratic Republic created in the fall. Europe was already divided prior to the Korean War. Soviet-type regimes were in power in all the countries lying between Germany and the USSR.

The Soviet Union and Europe

Why did the Soviet Union install, between 1945 and 1948, in Poland, Czechoslovakia, Hungary, Romania, Albania, and Bulgaria, governments under the domination or control of the Communists? Why did it precipitate a crisis in 1948 with the sole communist government which had

---

12. France's policy in 1945 no doubt contributed to the division of Germany. But conversely, it made it possible to avoid the creation of central German administrations more or less controlled, or influenced by the USSR, with power over the whole of Germany.

established itself without Soviet aid—that of Marshal Tito in Yugoslavia? Why did it create in its zone of Germany, as early as 1945, political parties, "popular" movements, and "central administrations," out of which a German government was formed in East Berlin in 1949, after the split with its wartime allies? Why did the USSR prefer *total* influence over a *portion* of Germany to *partial* influence over the *whole* of Germany?

The answer to these questions must be sought in the nature of the Soviet regime: unique in kind (because the first) and universal by its vocation, it based its power on a kind of scientism, the dialectics of "class warfare," which was its sole legitimation. It trusted neither movements of opinion, nor traditions, nor gratitude for services rendered. It was at its ease only if it enjoyed monopoly of word and action: within its frontiers by rigorous control over all manifestations or publications, beyond its frontiers by creating wherever possible regimes like itself. It was not only the desire for conquest which motivated Stalin in 1945, it was necessity. He was constrained to constrain if he wished to justify, and thereby to reinforce the power he wielded from Thuringia to the Pacific.

The United States and Europe

The Western Allies did not grasp this aspect of the situation in 1945. The English and Americans have often been reproached for having shown themselves as not only naive but blind at Yalta. One must however recognize the fact that the disappointments which followed on Yalta were not without effect: without the attempt to reach a settlement, without the almost immediate failure of this effort, would the leadership in Washington have taken, two years later, the decisive postwar change of course? When, in June 1947, General Marshall proposed to Europe the aid plan which radically transformed the situation and which, let us recall, was offered (not without mental reservations) to all European states including the Soviet Union, he transformed the situation in Europe. The Marshall Plan, to be sure, did not solve all the problems, but it salvaged just about everything that could be salvaged. Europe was divided, but the portion to the west once more had a future.

The United States kept their armed forces in Europe because after the Moscow Foreign Ministers' Conference (April–May 1947), it dawned on them that neither the German problem nor, consequently, the problem of Europe would be settled. The American military presence made it possible, in 1949, to provide the Atlantic Pact with a solid base, thanks to which western Europe was able not only to survive, but to revive. It was able to conceive the innovation known as the European Community based on reconciliation with Germany, to weather the crises of decolonization and in considerable measure to reconcile itself with its former overseas possessions.

We might be tempted to stop there, were this equilibrium between East and West based on agreements, or at least on a twofold consent, which was not the case. One of the long-term goals of the policy of the USSR is to bring about the withdrawal of the United States forces to the American continent. The various proposals on limitation of armaments or the denuclearization of Europe have no other goal. Even if each of the two returns home, one remains very near, whereas the other finds itself once again back on the other side of the Atlantic. This is what lies behind Moscow's slogan: *Europe, our common home,* which is to say: Europe without the Americans. Should they both withdraw, the Soviets, wherever they may go to, are still there. The American presence is indispensable because the Soviet presence is inescapable. How can we escape from this dilemma?

In Search of a Solution

One solution would be to stay as we are, to wait for more favorable circumstances and, so long as Germany (and with her, Europe) is divided, to live with the axiom: *No security for Europe without the Federal Republic of Germany; no security for the FRG without the United States.* This is doubtless the solution which will prevail. But one must try to go a little further.

No one knows what will come out of Mr. Gorbachev's reforms. But one sees that if they last, they will make a return to absolutist and devastating neo-Stalinism more difficult, both in the USSR and in the countries which Moscow (not without difficulty) controls. Should this be the case, we may ask ourselves what policy should be followed in order to favor such an evolution. One approach would be not to contemplate agreements on limitation of armaments in Europe without parallel action tending toward ending the political division of the old Continent. From this viewpoint, one can regret that an American-Soviet agreement on withdrawal of medium-range nuclear weapons was concluded in 1987 without any link to European policy as a whole. This was doubtless due to the fact that the latter doesn't exist. If it existed, it would consist in linking progress on limitation of armaments to progress on freedom of choice for countries between the USSR and western Europe, which might be spaced out, but which would reestablish conditions in Europe tending toward true peace.

For the Soviet Union, it would be a matter of achieving security based on assent of opinion among its allies, in other words, a security system protecting the freedom of choice of each ally on matters concerning its internal regime. Given the disproportion of strength between one of the allies and the others, such freedom would have limits, but it would nevertheless exist, and would give the USSR greater security than it achieves or has achieved by imposing communist regimes on countries which want no part of them and whose resistance is justified today by everything that is being revealed by the Soviet press, radio, and television about the regime directed by Stalin and, to a lesser degree, by his successors. When Gorbachev admits, as he did in Belgrade, that "no one possesses the monopoly of truth," and thus that the USSR, like Yugoslavia, "harbors no intentions of imposing on whomever it may be its own ideas on the evolution of societies,"[13] either this is hot air, or something must come of it. If this is really so, this result can be combined with arrangements concerning limitation of armaments. But on one condition! That the United States should continue to maintain armed forces on the European continent, because the whole security structure would collapse if one European power were to acquire overwhelming superiority in relation to all the others.

These suggestions, which do not even constitute outlines, have no other aim than to point the way, to encourage reflection on means of gradually erasing the consequences of the 1939–1945 war, which presupposes an equilibrium (hence negotiation on limitation of armaments), but also a sufficient degree of autonomy of decision so that every government should freely be able to associate itself with the negotiations without being obliged to defer to all the wishes of its closest and strongest neighbor.

Such prospects are very long term. All the more reason to think them over, to start discussing them now, and to stress that, pending their fulfillment, the present balance of forces must be upheld. All the more because since 1945 the insoluble German problem has lain at the heart of Europe. Nothing prevents the Western powers from calling for the reunification of Germany, as they have done for years. But calling for it will not achieve it. What one might propose

---

13. "Soviet-Yugoslav Communiqué, March 19, 1988," in *Izvestia,* March 19, 1988.

is to study, within the framework of the Atlantic alliance, various outlines of a gradual solution of the German question, to be conveyed to the USSR from the point of view of a return to peace in Europe. Several kinds of solution could be taken under consideration so long as they are based on the principles of freedom of communication and of circulation *(as broad as possible)* between the two German republics and so long as they might, in the long run, lead to a satisfactory solution, itself forming part of an overall European peace settlement.

Does this mean that one should contemplate another Yalta conference? That is another matter. It is a matter of seeing whether the current evolution in the USSR, which is far from having run its course, and whose long-term motivation we still do not know, could give some chance of success to the idea of a European settlement, moving forward by stages and maintaining the present balance of forces, but looking ahead toward something other than a *status quo,* perpetuating a division which is both unhealthy and dangerous. From the Western point of view, the two major difficulties are the German question and the necessity, for many years to come, of an American military presence in Europe. In fact, whatever the angle from which we examine them, we find ourselves faced with dilemmas difficult to resolve.

If the Yalta conference is a model we should not follow, one must, rather, envisage a negotiation of long duration, but nearer to reality than the Vienna discussions on "security and cooperation in Europe." The factor which justifies such an effort is the evolution of the USSR as we see it today: still ambiguous but not devoid of reality.

This calls for sustained effort, at a minimum over the final decade of this century, not another Yalta, a new Potsdam, or more Geneva conferences. Perhaps nothing will happen. But, for want of thinking about what might and should happen, we risk abdicating all control over the course of events—the good if these are confirmed, the bad if one wishes to confront them with effective resistance.

Not: *Get out of Yalta,* but: *Learn the lessons of Yalta!*

Appendix A

Text of the Communiqué of the Yalta Conference[1]

The Crimea Conference of the heads of the Governments of the United States of America, the United Kingdom, and the Union of Soviet Socialist Republics, which took place from Feb. 4 to 11, came to the following conclusions:

I. World Organization

It was decided:

1. That a United Nations conference on the proposed world organization should be summoned for Wednesday, 25 April, 1945, and should be held in the United States of America.

2. The nations to be invited to this conference should be:

1. Henry Steele Commager, ed., *Documents of American History*, 7th ed. (New York: Appleton-Century-Crofts, 1963), 488–493.

(a) the United Nations as they existed on 8 Feb., 1945; and

(b) Such of the Associated Nations as have declared war on the common enemy by 1 March, 1945. (For this purpose, by the term "Associated Nations" was meant the eight Associated Nations and Turkey.) When the conference on world organization is held, the delegates of the United Kingdom and United States of America will support a proposal to admit to original membership two Soviet Socialist Republics, i.e., the Ukraine and White Russia.

3. That the United States Government, on behalf of the three powers, should consult the Government of China and the French Provisional Government in regard to decisions taken at the present conference concerning the proposed world organization.

4. That the text of the invitation to be issued to all the nations which would take part in the United Nations conference should be as follows:

"The Government of the United States of America, on behalf of itself and of the Governments of the United Kingdom, the Union of Soviet Socialistic Republics and the Republic of China and of the Provisional Government of the French Republic, invite the Government of ———— to send representatives to a conference to be held on 25 April, 1945, or soon thereafter, at San Francisco, in the United States of America, to prepare a charter for a general international organization for the maintenance of international peace and security.

"The above-named Governments suggest that the conference consider as affording a basis for such a Charter the proposals for the establishment of a general international organization which were made public last October as a result of the Dumbarton Oaks conference and which have now been supplemented by the following provisions for Section C of Chapter VI:

C. Voting

"1. Each member of the Security Council should have one vote.

"2. Decisions of the Security Council on procedural matters should be made by an affirmative vote of seven members.

"3. Decisions of the Security Council on all matters should be made by an affirmative vote of seven members, including the concurring votes of the permanent members; provided that, in decisions under Chapter VIII, Section A and under the second sentence of Paragraph 1 of Chapter VIII, Section C, a party to a dispute should abstain from voting.

"Further information as to arrangements will be transmitted subsequently.

"In the event that the Government of ——— desires in advance of the conference to present views or comments concerning the proposals, the Government of the United States of America will be pleased to transmit such views and comments to the other participating Governments."

Territorial trusteeship:

It was agreed that the five nations which will have permanent seats on the Security Council should consult each other prior to the United Nations conference on the question of territorial trusteeship.

The acceptance of this recommendation is subject to its being made clear that territorial trusteeship will only apply to (a) existing mandates of the League of Nations; (b) territories detached from the enemy as a result of the present war; (c) any other territory which might voluntarily be placed under trusteeship; and (d) no discussion of actual territories is contemplated at the forthcoming United Nations conference or in the preliminary consultations, and it will be a matter for subsequent agreement which territories within the above categories will be placed under trusteeship.

[The section from this point to the next italicized note was published Feb. 13, 1945.]

II. Declaration on Liberated Europe

The following declaration has been approved:

The Premier of the Union of Soviet Socialist Republics, the Prime Minister of the United Kingdom and the President of the United States of America have consulted with each other in the common interests of the peoples of their countries and those of liberated Europe. They jointly declare their mutual agreement to concert during the temporary period of instability in liberated Europe the policies of their three Governments in assisting the peoples liberated from the domination of Nazi Germany and the peoples of the former Axis satellite states of Europe to solve by democratic means their pressing political and economic problems.

The establishment of order in Europe and the rebuilding of national economic life must be achieved by processes which will enable the liberated peoples to destroy the last vestiges of nazism and fascism and to create democratic institutions of their own choice. This is a principle of the Atlantic Charter—the right of all peoples to choose the form of government under which they will live—the restoration of sovereign rights and self-government to those peoples who have been forcibly deprived of them by the aggressor nations.

To foster the conditions in which the liberated peoples may exercise these rights, the three Governments will jointly assist the people in any European liberated state or former Axis satellite state in Europe where, in their judgment conditions require, (a) to establish conditions of internal peace; (b) to carry out emergency measures for the relief of distressed peoples; (c) to form interim governmental authorities broadly representative of all democratic elements in the population and pledged to the earliest possible establishment through free elections of Governments responsive to the will of the people; and (d) to facilitate where necessary the holding of such elections.

The three Governments will consult the other United Nations and provisional authorities or other Governments in Europe when matters of direct interest to them are under consideration.

When, in the opinion of the three Governments, conditions in any European liberated state or any former Axis satellite state in Europe make such action necessary, they will immediately consult together on the measures necessary to discharge the joint responsibilities set forth in this declaration.

By this declaration we reaffirm our faith in the principles of the Atlantic Charter, our pledge in the Declaration by the United Nations and our determination to build in cooperation with other peace-loving nations world order, under law, dedicated to peace, security, freedom and general well-being of all mankind.

In issuing this declaration, the three powers express the hope that the Provisional Government of the French Republic may be associated with them in the procedure suggested.

[*Here ends the previously published part of this section of the agreements.*]

III. Dismemberment of Germany

It was agreed that Article 12 (a) of the Surrender Terms for Germany should be amended to read as follows:

"The United Kingdom, the United States of America and the Union of Soviet Socialist Republics shall possess supreme authority with respect to Germany. In the exercise of such authority they will take such steps, including the complete disarmament, demilitarization and dismemberment of Germany as they deem requisite for future peace and security."

The study of the procedure of the dismemberment of Germany was referred to a committee consisting of Mr. [Anthony] Eden [their Foreign Secretary] (chairman), Mr. [John] Winant [of the United States] and Mr. [Fedor T.] Gusev. This body would consider the desirability of associating with it a French representative.

IV. Zone of Occupation for the French and Control Council for Germany

It was agreed that a zone in Germany, to be occupied by the French forces, should be allocated to France. This zone would be formed out of the British and American zones and its extent would be settled by the British and Americans in consultation with the French Provisional Government.

It was also agreed that the French Provisional Government should be invited to become a member of the Allied Control Council for Germany.

V. Reparation

The following protocol has been approved:

Protocol

On the Talks Between the Heads of Three Governments at the Crimean Conference on the Question of the German Reparations in Kind

1. Germany must pay in kind for the losses caused by

her to the Allied nations in the course of the war. Reparations are to be received in the first instance by those countries which have borne the main burden of the war, have suffered the heaviest losses and have organized victory over the enemy.

2. Reparations in kind is to be exacted from Germany in three following forms:

(a) Removals within two years from the surrender of Germany or the cessation of organized resistance from the national wealth of Germany located on the territory of Germany herself as well as outside her territory (equipment, machine tools, ships, rolling stock, Germany investments abroad, shares of industrial, transport and other enterprises in Germany, etc.), these removals to be carried out chiefly for the purpose of destroying the war potential of Germany.

(b) Annual deliveries of goods from current production for a period to be fixed.

(c) Use of German labor.

3. For the working out on the above principles of a detailed plan for exaction of reparation from Germany an Allied reparations commission will be set up in Moscow. It will consist of three representatives—one from the Union of Soviet Socialist Republics, one from the United Kingdom and one from the United States of America.

4. With regard to the fixing of the total sum of the reparation as well as the distribution of it among the countries which suffered from the German aggression, the Soviet and American delegations agreed as follows:

"The Moscow reparation commission should take in its initial studies as a basis for discussion the suggestion of the Soviet Government that the total sum of the reparation in accordance with the points (a) and (b) of the Paragraph 2 should be 20 billion dollars and that 50 per cent of it should go to the Union of Soviet Socialist Republics."

The British delegation was of the opinion that, pending consideration of the reparation question by the Moscow reparation commission, no figures of reparation should be mentioned.

The above Soviet-American proposal has been passed to the Moscow reparation commission as one of the proposals to be considered by the commission.

VI. Major War Criminals

The conference agreed that the question of the major war criminals should be the subject of inquiry by the three Foreign Secretaries for report in due course after the close of the conference.

[*The section from this point to the next italicized note was published Feb. 13, 1945.*]

VII. Poland

The following declaration on Poland was agreed by the conference:

"A new situation has been created in Poland as a result of her complete liberation by the Red Army. This calls for the establishment of a Polish Provisional Government which can be more broadly based than was possible before the recent liberation of the western part of Poland. The Provisional Government which is now functioning in Poland should therefore be reorganized on a broader democratic basis with the inclusion of democratic leaders from Poland itself and from Poles abroad. This new Government should then be called the Polish Provisional Government of National Unity.

"M. Molotov, Mr. Harriman and Sir A. Clark Kerr are authorized as a commission to consult in the first instance in Moscow with members of the present Provisional Government and with other Polish democratic leaders from within Poland and from abroad, with a view to the reorganization of the present Government along the above lines. This Polish Provisional Government of National Unity shall be pledged to the holding of free and unfettered elections as soon as possible on the basis of universal suffrage and secret ballot. In these elections all democratic and anti-Nazi parties shall have the right to take part and to put forward candidates.

"When a Polish Provisional Government of National Unity has been properly formed in conformity with the above, the Government of the U.S.S.R., which now maintains diplomatic relations with the present Provisional Government of Poland, and the Government of the United Kingdom and the Government of the United States of America will establish diplomatic relations with the new Polish Provisional Government of National Unity, and will exchange Ambassadors by whose reports the respective Governments will be kept informed about the situation in Poland.

"The three heads of Government consider that the eastern frontier of Poland should follow the Curzon Line with digressions from it in some regions of five to eight kilometers in favor of Poland. They recognize that Poland must receive substantial accessions of territory in the north and west. They feel that the opinion of the new Polish Provisional Government of National Unity should be sought in due course of the extent of these accessions and that the final delimitation of the western frontier of Poland should thereafter await the peace conference."

VIII. Yugoslavia

It was agreed to recommend to Marshal Tito and to Dr. [Ivan] Subasitch:

(a) That the Tito-Subasitch agreement should immediately be put into effect and a new Government formed on the basis of the agreement.

(b) That as soon as the new Government has been formed it should declare:

(I) That the Anti-Fascist Assembly of the National Liberation (AVNOJ) will be extended to include members of the last Yugoslav Skupstina who have not compromised themselves by collaboration with the enemy, thus forming a body to be known as a temporary Parliament and

(II) That legislative acts passed by the Anti-Fascist Assembly of National Liberation (AVNOJ) will be subject to subsequent ratification by a Constituent Assembly; and that this statement should be published in the communiqué of the conference.

[*Here ends the previously published section of the agreements.*]

IX. Italo-Yugoslav Frontier— Italo-Austrian Frontier

Notes on these subjects were put in by the British delegation, and the American and Soviet delegations agreed to consider them and give their views later.

X. Yugoslav-Bulgarian Relations

There was an exchange of views between the Foreign Secretaries on the question of the desirability of a Yugoslav-Bulgarian pact of alliance. The question at issue was whether a state still under an armistice regime could be allowed to enter into a treaty with another state. Mr. Eden suggested that the Bulgarian and Yugoslav Governments should be informed that this could not be approved. Mr. Stettinius suggested that the British and American Ambassadors should discuss the matter further with Mr. Molotov in Moscow. Mr. Molotov agreed with the proposal of Mr. Stettinius.

XI. Southeastern Europe

The British delegation put in notes for the consideration of their colleagues on the following subjects:

(a) The Control Commission in Bulgaria.

(b) Greek claims upon Bulgaria, more particularly with reference to reparations.

(c) Oil equipment in Rumania.

XII. Iran

Mr. Eden, Mr. Stettinius and Mr. Molotov exchanged views on the situation in Iran. It was agreed that this matter should be pursued through the diplomatic channel.

[*The section from this point to the next italicized note was published Feb. 13, 1945.*]

XIII. Meetings of the Three Foreign Secretaries

The conference agreed that permanent machinery should be set up for consultation between the three Foreign Secretaries; they should meet as often as necessary, probably about every three or four months.

These meetings will be held in rotation in the three capitals, the first meeting being held in London.

[*Here ends the previously published section of the agreements.*]

XIV. The Montreux Convention and the Straits

It was agreed that at the next meeting of the three Foreign Secretaries to be held in London, they should consider proposals which it was understood the Soviet Government would put forward in relation to the Montreux Convention, and report to their Governments. The Turkish Government should be informed at the appropriate moment.

The foregoing protocol was approved and signed by the three Foreign Secretaries at the Crimean Conference Feb. 11, 1945.

> E. R. Stettinius Jr.
> M. Molotov
> Anthony Eden

Agreement Regarding Japan

The leaders of the three great powers—the Soviet Union, the United States of America and Great Britain—have agreed that in two or three months after Germany has surrendered and the war in Europe has terminated, the Soviet Union shall enter into the war against Japan on the side of the Allies on condition that:

1. The status quo in Outer Mongolia (the Mongolian People's Republic) shall be preserved;

2. The former rights of Russia violated by the treacherous attack of Japan in 1904 shall be restored, viz.:

(a) The southern part of Sakhalin as well as the islands adjacent to it shall be returned to the Soviet Union;

(b) The commercial port of Dairen shall be internationalized, the pre-eminent interests of the Soviet Union in this port being safeguarded, and the lease of Port Arthur as a naval base of the U.S.S.R. restored;

(c) The Chinese-Eastern Railroad and the South Manchurian Railroad, which provide an outlet to Dairen, shall be jointly operated by the establishment of a joint Soviet-Chinese company, it being understood that the pre-eminent interests of the Soviet Union shall be safeguarded and that China shall retain full sovereignty in Manchuria;

3. The Kurile Islands shall be handed over to the Soviet Union.

It is understood that the agreement concerning Outer Mongolia and the ports and railroads referred to above will require concurrence of Generalissimo Chiang Kai-shek. The President will take measures in order to obtain this concurrence on advice from Marshal Stalin.

The heads of the three great powers have agreed that these claims of the Soviet Union shall be unquestionably fulfilled after Japan has been defeated.

For its part, the Soviet Union expresses its readiness to conclude with the National Government of China a pact of friendship and alliance between the U.S.S.R. and China in order to render assistance to China with its armed forces for the purpose of liberating China from the Japanese yoke.

Joseph V. Stalin
Franklin D. Roosevelt
Winston S. Churchill

February 11, 1945.

Appendix B

Part 1:
Exchange of Letters Between
Roosevelt and Stalin
(April 1945)[1]

A. Roosevelt to Stalin
(April 5, 1945)

Personal and Top Secret for Marshal Stalin from President Roosevelt

I have received with astonishment your message of April 3 containing an allegation that arrangements which were made between Field Marshals Alexander and Kesselring at Berne "permitted the Anglo-American troops to

1. *The Secret History of World War II: The Ultra-Secret Wartime Letters and Cables of Roosevelt, Stalin and Churchill.* (New York: Richardson & Steirman, 1986), 264–268.

advance to the East and the Anglo-Americans promised in return to ease for the Germans the peace terms."

In my previous messages to you in regard to the attempts made in Berne to arrange a conference to discuss a surrender of the German army in Italy I have told you that: (1) No negotiations were held in Berne, (2) The meeting had no political implications whatever, (3) In any surrender of the enemy army in Italy, there would be no violation of our agreed principle of unconditional surrender, (4) Soviet officers would be welcomed at any meeting that might be arranged to discuss surrender.

For the advantage of our common war effort against Germany, which today gives excellent promise of an early success in a disintegration of the German armies, I must continue to assume that you have the same high confidence in my truthfulness and reliability that I have always had in yours.

I have also a full appreciation of the effect your gallant army has had in making possible a crossing of the Rhine by the forces under General Eisenhower and the effect that your forces will have hereafter on the eventual collapse of the German resistance to our combined attacks.

I have complete confidence in General Eisenhower and know that he certainly would inform me before entering into any agreement with the Germans. He is instructed to demand and will demand unconditional surrender of enemy troops that may be defeated on his front. Our advances on the Western Front are due to military action. Their speed has been attributable mainly to the terrific impact of our air power resulting in destruction of German communications, and to the fact that Eisenhower was able to cripple the bulk of the German forces on the Western Front while they were still west of the Rhine.

I am certain that there were no negotiations in Berne at any time, and I feel that your information to that effect must have come from German sources which have made persistent efforts to create dissension between us in order to escape in some measure responsibility for their war crimes. If that was Wolff's purpose in Berne, your message proves that he has had some success.

With a confidence in your belief in my personal reliability and in my determination to bring about, together with you, an unconditional surrender of the Nazis, it is astonishing that a belief seems to have reached the Soviet Government that I have entered into an agreement with the enemy without first obtaining your full agreement.

Finally I would say this; it would be one of the great tragedies of history if, at the very moment of the victory now within our grasp, such distrust, such lack of faith should prejudice the entire undertaking after the colossal losses of life, material and treasure involved.

Frankly, I cannot avoid a feeling of bitter resentment toward your informers, whoever they are, for such vile misrepresentations of my actions or those of my trusted subordinates.

Stalin's Reply
(April 7, 1945)

Personal and Secret from Premier J. V. Stalin to the President, Mr. F. Roosevelt

I have received your message of April 5.

In my message of April 3, the point was not about integrity or trustworthiness. I have never doubted your integrity or trustworthiness, just as I have never questioned the integrity or trustworthiness of Mr. Churchill. My point is that in the course of our correspondence a difference of views has arisen over what an Ally may permit himself with regard to another and what he may not. We Russians believe that, in view of the present situation on the fronts, a

situation in which the enemy is faced with inevitable surrender, whenever the representatives of one of the Allies meet
the Germans to discuss surrender terms, the representatives of the other Ally should be enabled to take part in the
meeting. That is absolutely necessary, at least when the
other Ally seeks participation in the meeting. The Americans and British, however, have a different opinion: they
hold that the Russian point of view is wrong. For that reason they have denied the Russians the right to be present
at the meeting with the Germans in Switzerland. I have
already written to you, and I see no harm in repeating that,
given a similar situation, the Russians would never have
denied the Americans and British the right to attend such
a meeting. I still consider the Russian point of view to be
the only correct one, because it precludes mutual suspicions and gives the enemy no chance to sow distrust between us.

2. It is hard to agree that the absence of German resistance on the Western Front is due solely to the fact that
they have been beaten. The Germans have 147 divisions on
the Eastern Front. They could safely withdraw from 15 to
20 divisions from the Eastern Front to aid their forces on
the Western Front. Yet they have not done so, nor are they
doing so. They are fighting desperately against the Russians for Zemlenice, an obscure station in Czechoslovakia,
which they need just as much as a dead man needs a poul-
tice, but they surrender without any resistance such important towns in the heart of Germany as Osnabrück, Mann-
heim, and Kassel. You will admit that this behavior on the
part of the Germans is more than strange and unaccounta-
ble.

3. As regards those who supply my information, I can
assure you that they are honest and unassuming people
who carry out their duties conscientiously and who have no
intention of affronting anybody. They have been tested in
action on numerous occasions. Judge for yourself. In Feb-

ruary General Marshall made available to the General Staff of the Soviet troops a number of important reports in which he, citing data in his possession, warned the Russians that in March the Germans were planning two serious counter-blows on the Eastern Front; one from Pomerania towards Thorn, the other from the Moravská Ostrava area towards Lódź. It turned out, however, that the main German blow had been prepared and delivered not in the areas mentioned above, but in an entirely different area; namely, in the Lake Balaton area, southwest of Budapest. The Germans, as we now know, had concentrated 35 divisions in the area, 11 of them armored. This, with its great concentration of armor, was one of the heaviest blows of the war, Marshal Tolbukhin succeeded first in warding off disaster and then in smashing the Germans, and was able to do so also because my informants had disclosed—true, with some delay—the plan for the main German blow and immediately apprised Marshal Tolbukhin. Thus I had yet another opportunity to satisfy myself as to the reliability and soundness of my sources of information.

For your guidance in this matter, I enclose a letter sent by Army General Antonov, Chief of Staff of the Red Army, to Major-General Deane.

April 7, 1945
Copy.

Appendix B

Part 2:
Exchange of Letters Between Churchill and Stalin
(April–May 1945)[1]

Churchill to Stalin
(April 28, 1945)

. . . we are all shocked that you should think we would work for a Polish Government hostile to the U.S.S.R. This is the opposite of our policy. But it was on account of Poland that the British went to war with Germany in 1939. We saw in the Nazi treatment of Poland a symbol of Hitler's vile and

1. Ministry of Foreign Affairs of the U.S.S.R., *Correspondence Between the Chairman of the Council of Ministers of the U.S.S.R. and the Presidents of the U.S.A. and the Prime Ministers of Great Britain during the Great Patriotic War of 1941–1945*, vol. 1. *Correspondence with Winston S. Churchill and Clement R. Attlee (July 1941–November 1945)* (Moscow: Foreign Languages Publishing House, 1957), 225–227 and 341–344.

wicked lust of conquest and subjugation, and his invasion of Poland was the spark that fired the mine. The British people do not, as is sometimes thought, go to war for calculation, but for sentiment. They had a feeling, which grew up in the years, that with all Hitler's encroachments and preparations he was a danger to our country and to the liberties which we prize in Europe and when after Munich he broke his word so shamefully about Czechoslovakia even the extremely peace-loving Chamberlain gave our guarantee against Hitler to Poland. When that guarantee was invoked by the German invasion of Poland the whole nation went to war with Hitler, unprepared as we were. There was a flame in the hearts of men like that which swept your people in their noble defence of their country from a treacherous, brutal, and as at one time it almost seemed, overwhelming German attack. This British flame burns still among all classes and parties in this island and in its self-governing Dominions, and they can never feel this war will have ended rightly unless Poland has a fair deal in the full sense of sovereignty, independence and freedom on a basis of friendship with Russia. It was on this that I thought we had agreed at Yalta.

7. Side by side with this strong sentiment for the rights of Poland, which I believe is shared in at least as strong a degree throughout the United States, there has grown up throughout the English-speaking world a very warm and deep desire to be friends on equal and honourable terms with the mighty Russian Soviet Republic and to work with you, making allowances for our different systems of thought and government, in the long and bright years for all the world which we three Powers alone can make together. I, who in my years of great responsibility, have worked methodically for this unity, will certainly continue to do so by every means in my power, and in particular I can assure you that we in Great Britain would not work for

or tolerate a Polish Government unfriendly to Russia. Neither could we recognise a Polish Government that did not truly correspond to the description in our joint declaration at Yalta with proper regard for the rights of the individual as we understand these matters in the Western world.

8. With regard to your reference to Greece and Belgium, I recognise the consideration which you gave me when we had to intervene with heavy armed forces to quell the E.A.M.-E.L.A.S. attack upon the centre of government in Athens. We have given repeated instructions that your interest in Roumania and Bulgaria is to be recognised as predominant. We cannot however be excluded altogether, and we dislike being treated by your subordinates in these countries so differently from the kind manner in which we at the top are always treated by you. In Greece we seek nothing but her friendship, which is of long duration, and desire only her independence and integrity. But we have no intention of trying to decide whether she is to be a monarchy or a republic. Our only policy there is to restore matters to normal as quickly as possible and to hold fair and free elections, I hope within the next four or five months. These elections will decide the régime and later on the constitution. The will of the people expressed in conditions of freedom and universal franchise must prevail; that is our root principle. If the Greeks were to decide for a republic it would not affect our relations with them. We will use our influence with the Greek Government to invite Russian representatives to come and see freely what is going on in Greece, and at the elections I hope that there will be Russian, American and British Commissioners at large in the country to make sure that there is no intimidation or other frustration of freedom of choice of the people between the different parties who will be contending. After that our work in Greece may well be done.

9. As to Belgium we have no conditions to demand

though . . . we hope they will, under whatever form of government they adopt by popular decision, come into a general system of resistance to prevent Germany striking westward. Belgium, like Poland, is a theatre of war and corridor of communication, and everyone must recognise the force of these considerations, without which the great armies cannot operate.

10. . . . it is quite true that about Poland we have reached a definite line of action with the Americans. This is because we agree naturally upon the subject, and both sincerely feel we have been rather ill-treated about the way the matter has been handled since the Crimea Conference. No doubt these things seem different when looked at from the opposite point of view. But we are absolutely agreed that the pledge we have given for a sovereign, free, independent Poland with a government fully and adequately representing all democratic elements among the Poles, is for us a matter of honour and duty. I do not think there is the slightest chance of any change in the attitude of our two Powers, and when we are agreed we are bound to say so. After all, we have joined with you, largely on my original initiative early in 1944, in proclaiming the Polish-Russian frontier which you desired, namely the Curzon Line including Lvov for Russia. We think you ought to meet us with regard to the other half of the policy which you equally with us have proclaimed, namely the sovereignty, independence and freedom of Poland, provided it is a Poland friendly to Russia. . . .

11. Also difficulties arise at the present moment because all sorts of stories are brought out of Poland which are eagerly listened to by many members of Parliament and which at any time may be violently raised in Parliament or the press in spite of my deprecating such action and on which M. Molotov will vouchsafe us no information at all in spite of repeated requests. *For instance, there is talk of fifteen*

Poles who were said to have met the Russian authorities for discussion over four weeks ago, and of M. Witos about whom there has been a similar, but more recent report; and there are many other statements of deportations, etc. [2] How can I contradict such complaints when you give me no information whatever and when neither I nor the Americans are allowed to send anyone into Poland to find out for themselves the true state of affairs? There is no part of our occupied or liberated territory into which you are not free to send delegations, and people do not see why you should have any reasons against similar visits by British delegations to foreign countries liberated by you.

12. There is not much comfort in looking into a future where you and the countries you dominate, plus the Communist parties in many other States, are all drawn up on one side, and those who rally to the English-speaking nations and their Associates or Dominions are on the other. It is quite obvious that their quarrel would tear the world to pieces and that all of us leading men on either side who had anything to do with that would be shamed before history. Even embarking on a long period of suspicions, of abuse and counter-abuse and of opposing policies would be a disaster hampering the great developments of world prosperity for the masses which are attainable only by our trinity. I hope there is no word or phrase in this outpouring of my heart to you which unwittingly gives offence. If so, let me know. But do not, I beg you, my friend Stalin, underrate the divergencies which are opening about matters which you may think are small to us but which are symbolic of the way the English-speaking democracies look at life.

April 28th, 1945

2. Italics are Churchill's.

Stalin's Reply to Churchill
(May 4, 1945)

I am in receipt of your message of April 28 on the Polish question.

I must say that I cannot accept the arguments put forward in support of your stand.

You are inclined to regard the proposal that the Yugoslav precedent be accepted as a model for Poland as renunciation of the procedure agreed between us for setting up a Polish Government of National Unity. I cannot agree with you. I think that the Yugoslav precedent is important first of all because it points the way to the most suitable and practical solution of the problem of forming a new United Government based on the governmental agency at present exercising state power in the country.

It is quite obvious that, unless the Provisional Government now functioning in Poland and enjoying the support and trust of a majority of the Polish people is taken as a basis for a future Government of National Unity, it will be impossible to count on successful fulfilment of the task set us by the Crimea Conference.

2. I cannot subscribe to that part of your considerations on Greece where you suggest three-Power control over the elections. Such control over the people of an allied country would of necessity be assessed as an affront and gross interference in their internal affairs. Such control is out of place in relation to former satellite countries which subsequently declared war on Germany and ranged themselves with the Allies, as demonstrated by electoral experience, for example, in Finland, where the election was held without outside interference and yielded positive results.

Your comments on Belgium and Poland as war theatres and communication corridors are perfectly justified. As regards Poland, it is her being a neighbour of the Soviet Union that makes it essential for a future Polish

Government to seek in practice friendly relations between Poland and the U.S.S.R., which is also in the interests of the other freedom-loving nations. This circumstance, too, speaks for the Yugoslav precedent. The United Nations are interested in constant and durable friendship between the U.S.S.R. and Poland. Hence we cannot acquiesce in the attempts that are being made to involve in the forming of a future Polish Government people who, to quote you, "are not fundamentally anti-Russian," or to bar from participation only those who, in your view, are "extreme people unfriendly to Russia." Neither one nor the other can satisfy us. We insist, and shall continue to insist, that only people who have demonstrated by deeds their friendly attitude to the Soviet Union, who are willing honestly and sincerely to cooperate with the Soviet state, should be consulted on the formation of a future Polish Government.

3. I must deal specially with paragraph 11 of your message concerning the difficulties arising from rumours about the arrest of 15 Poles, about deportations, etc.

I am able to inform you that the group of Poles mentioned by you comprises 16, not 15, persons. The group is headed by the well-known General Okulicki. The British information services maintain a deliberate silence, in view of his particular odiousness, about this Polish General, who, along with the 15 other Poles, has "disappeared." But we have no intention of being silent about the matter. This group of 16, led by General Okulicki, has been arrested by the military authorities of the Soviet front and is undergoing investigation in Moscow. General Okulicki's group, in the first place General Okulicki himself, is charged with preparing and carrying out subversive activities behind the lines of the Red Army, subversion which has taken a toll of over a hundred Red Army soldiers and officers; the group is also charged with keeping illegal radio-transmitters in the rear of our troops, which is prohibited by law. All, or part of them—depending on the outcome of the investigation—will be tried. That is how the Red Army is forced to protect its units and its rear lines against saboteurs and those who create disorder.

The British information services are spreading rumours about the murder or shooting of Poles in Siedlce. The report is a fabrication from beginning to end and has, apparently, been concocted by Arciszewski's agents.

4. It appears from your message that you are unwilling to consider the Polish Provisional Government as a basis for a future Government of National Unity, or to accord it the place in that Government to which it is entitled. I must say frankly that this attitude precludes the possibility of an agreed decision on the Polish question.

May 4, 1945

Bibliography

Allied Relations During the War (1941–1945)

Duroselle, J. B. *De Wilson à Roosevelt, Politique extérieure des États Unis, 1913–1945.* Paris: Armand Colin, 1960.

Feis, Herbert. *Roosevelt, Stalin: The War They Waged, the Peace They Sought.* Princeton, N.J.: Princeton University Press, 1957.

Fontaine, André. *Histoire de la guerre froide,* 2 vols. Paris: Fayard, 1965.

Gaddis, John L. *The United States and the Origins of the Cold War, 1941–1947.* New York: Columbia University Press, 1972.

Michel, Henri. *La Seconde Guerre mondiale,* 2 vols. Paris: Presses Universitaires de France, 1968–1969.

Ross, Graham. *The Foreign Office and the Kremlin, British Documents on Anglo-Soviet Relations, 1941–1945.* Cambridge, England: Cambridge University Press, 1984.

Ulman, Adam J. *Expansion and Coexistence, The History of Soviet Foreign Policy, 1917–1967.* London: Secker & Warburg, 1968.

Woodward, Llewellyn (Sir). *British Foreign Policy in the Second World War,* 5 vols. London: HMS Office, 1971–1976.

The Crimean Conference

Bohlen, C. E. *Witness to History, 1929–1969.* New York: Norton & Co., 1973.

Byrnes, J. F. *Speaking Frankly.* New York: Harper & Brothers, 1958.

The Conferences at Malta and Yalta. Diplomatic Papers. Washington, D.C.: Government Printing Office, 1955.

Conte, A. *Yalta ou le partage du monde.* Paris: Robert Laffont, 1966.

Divine, R. A. *Roosevelt and World War II.* Baltimore, Md.: Johns Hopkins University Press, 1969.

Eden, A. (Earl of Avon). *The Eden Memoirs. The Reckoning.* London: Cassell, 1965.

Funk, A. *De Yalta à Potsdam.* Brussels: Éditions Complexe, 1982.

Harriman, A., and E. Abel. *Special Envoy to Churchill and Stalin, 1941–1946.* New York: Random House, 1975.

Mastny, V. *Russia's Road to the Cold War.* New York: Columbia University Press, 1979.

Mosely, P. E. *The Kremlin and World Politics,* New York: Vintage Books, 1960.

Senarclens, P. de. *Yalta.* Paris: Universitaires de France, 1984.

Shaver, Clemens Diane. *Yalta.* New York: Oxford University Press, 1970. (Contains a very complete bibliography.)

Sherwood, Robert E. *Roosevelt and Hopkins, An Intimate History.* New York: Harper & Brothers, 1948.

Snell, J. L. *The Meaning of Yalta.* Baton Rouge: Louisiana State University Press, 1956.

Stettinius, Edward R. *Roosevelt and the Russians: The Yalta Conference.* New York: Doubleday and Co., 1949.

Tinguy, Anne de. *Les relations Soviéto-Américaines.* Paris: Presses Universitaires de France, 1987.

Noteworthy Russian-language documents have been published in the series *Relations: British-Soviet,* 2 vols., 1983 (cf. Chapt. 2, n. 3, 20); *American-Soviet,* 2 vols., 1984 (cf. Chapt. 6, n. 7, 89); *French-Soviet,* 2 vols., 1984 (cf. Chapt. 2, n. 15, 28). See also Gromyko, Andrei A. *Memoirs (Pamiatnoe),* 2 vols. Moscow, 1988, especially vol. 1, Chapt. 4, "Tehran, Yalta, Potsdam."

Index

149

About the Author

As a young diplomat, Jean Laloy was interpreter for General de Gaulle in December 1944 during the first conversations with Stalin. Since then he has been continuously active in French foreign affairs, at the Quai d'Orsay, as an ambassador, as a leading scholar of Eastern Europe, and as the author of several important books about the USSR. He is widely known as one of the truly great specialists on the Soviet Union.